Exporting For
Small And Medium-Sized Firms

A practial guide for new exporters

Exporting For Small And Medium Sized Firms

A practical guide for new exporters

DANIEL ENET

Cartoons by Mick Davies
Translated by Denise Burton

BUSINESS BOOKS
COMMUNICA - EUROPA

ISBN 0 220 66329 7

Typesetting by TNR Productions, London

Printed in Great Britain
at the Alden Press, Oxford.

Contents

Foreword

Eighty per cent of British exports are carried out by 20 per cent of British firms. Once again, the rule of 80/20 is proved correct. The reason for this is that few companies really understand the advantages that exporting holds and above all, the ways in which the small and medium-sized companies can approach exporting. Although many small and medium-sized companies do in fact achieve some sales abroad and have some kind of an export department, they often think that exporting is just for the prestige it can bring and that it is not a profitable exercise.

Even though small and medium-sized companies barely exist on the international market, their products usually are subcontracted out to the giants of the exporting sector. Although it is true that small and medium-sized companies often hesitate to venture on to foreign markets, it must be remembered that credit squeezes and the dangers of too great a dependence on banks, do nothing to encourage them to do otherwise.

However, the government has now grasped the fact that the small and medium-sized company could play an important part in exporting. Large companies are hampered by heavy administrative costs and high overheads, and are gradually being replaced by small and medium-sized companies which are able to react quickly to different situations and which can put competitively priced goods onto the international market.

The government provides many forms of assistance to exporting firms through the BOTB (British Overseas Trade Board), ECGD (Export Credits Guarantee Department) etc.; purchasers' credits, suppliers' credits, export pre-financing, and almost total elimination of the risks of non-payment and of political problems. Although a large company has the resources to find out about such schemes, the small and medium-sized company often suffers from a lack of such information. Today it is up to the company to go out and inform itself. Trade associations, Chambers of Commerce, banks, the Department of Trade and Industry are there to provide the exporter, and above all, the small and medium-sized company, with this kind of information.

Once this information has been obtained it must be used effectively. As Gerard Le Pan de Ligny points out in his book on business trips 'to export one must go to see the buyer before the sale, during the sale and after the sale'. The exporter will not be able to find this information in his office nor will he be able to sell from his office.

Effective exporting relies on expertise — in international trade, customs, preparation on contracts, negotiation, market analysis, profit margins, foreign languages, understanding different attitudes . . . in other words the expertise of exporting!

In this book we are particularly concerned with helping small and medium-sized companies which usually only have an embryonic or even non-existent export department.

To do this we shall deal with the following points:

— methods of finding out the necessary information,

— how to use the information obtained, taking into account their basic aim: to sell abroad,

— the principal indicators essential to the success of any export policy.

Chapter 1

Exporting Within the Firm

1.1 Exporting. Its role within the firm

1.1.1 A larger market
1.1.2 Improved sales distribution
1.1.3 A way of fighting monetary fluctuations
1.1.4 A marketing tool
1.1.5 Securing investment

1.2 Structure of exports

1.2.1 Which marketing method to adopt
1.2.2 Examples of flow diagrams for an export department

1.3 Operation of an export department

1.3.1 Personnel
1.3.2 The constituents of an export department

Chapter 1

1.1 Exporting. Its role within the firm.

A great many small and medium-sized firms could export but most of them hesitate to do so. It is the foreign customer who buys and not the national company that sells. There is a great difference between selling abroad and really exporting. The dictionary definition of the verb 'to export' is 'to send commodities from one country to another'. However, it goes without saying that it also means selling goods abroad. Therefore, the role of exporting is not to bring prestige to the company but to help it increase its turnover. The advantages of exporting are as follows.

1.1.1 A larger market

Although the UK represents a market of 60 million people, Europe represents a market of 650 million and the whole world more than 3,000 million. Even taking into account that not every person can be a possible customer it is still true that the domestic market represents only a minute part of the world market. Therefore, a company which does not export is deliberately closing itself off from its principal markets. It is obvious that this market must be divided up into sectors so that it can be dealt with efficiently and rationally. This can be effected geographically or qualitatively, and one need not automatically limit oneself to existing national frontiers.

Exporting offers limitless possibilities. It tests the quality of the product concerned and can improve the company's management performance because of the more even and rational distribution of sales achieved.

It also enables one to be prepared for foreign competition in one's own market by using retaliation. The exporter can attack his competitor's market if his own is being attacked.

1.1.2 Improved sales distribution

The export sales curve does not always show the same fluctuations as the domestic sales curve. Taking into account different seasons and customs (natural or otherwise) a product whose peak sales period is the beginning of the year in Great Britain, may experience its peak sales period at the end of the year abroad, or vice versa. This is usually the case with seasonal products.

By means of the figures on page 5 it is easy to see that a company can control and spread out its production costs by distributing its sales more evenly throughout the year. A monthly summary of domestic sales for a whole year (Figure 2) shows a sharp fall in sales from July onwards. If, as the figure indicates, the domestic turnover in Great Britain is £585,000, the average sales for the month will be £48,750. Suppose that this industrial concern gears itself both from the manpower and equipment points of view to this turnover, various administrative problems will quickly arise. In the first half of the year (shown by the dotted area on the figure) the company will be over-producing. However, its sales team will be working below capacity and it will not be able to take any orders without allowing for considerable delays in delivery. A reduction in the number of salesmen, (practically an impossibility) or an increase in its production potential would therefore become necessary. Overtime by the production staff, or a temporary increase in the number of staff in order to cope with this demand, would considerably increase the retail price of the manufactured article, followed by profit margin cuts. However, in the second half of the year, the company will be working to full capacity and its machine shop will not be in use full-time. The higher hourly machine cost will result in an increase in the cost price and therefore in the selling price: so, there is a risk of producing non-competitive manufactured articles. During this period the sales team would be insufficient, the company would also stockpile and manufacture more during the slack period. One must also bear in mind that the cost of having capital tied up together with the generally high interest rates, would result in another effective loss.

FIGURE 1. EXPORT SALES

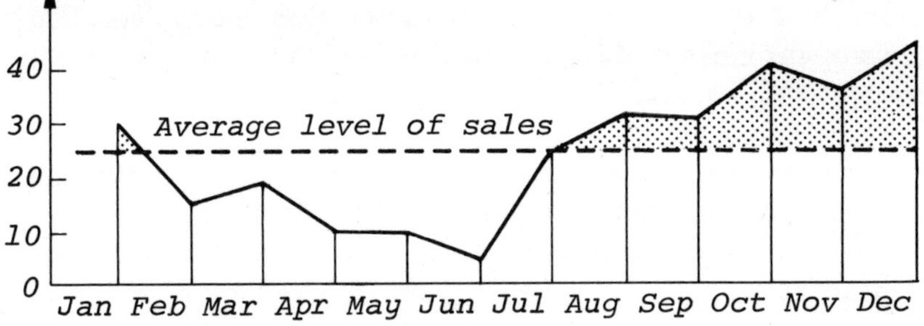

FIGURE 2. DOMESTIC SALES

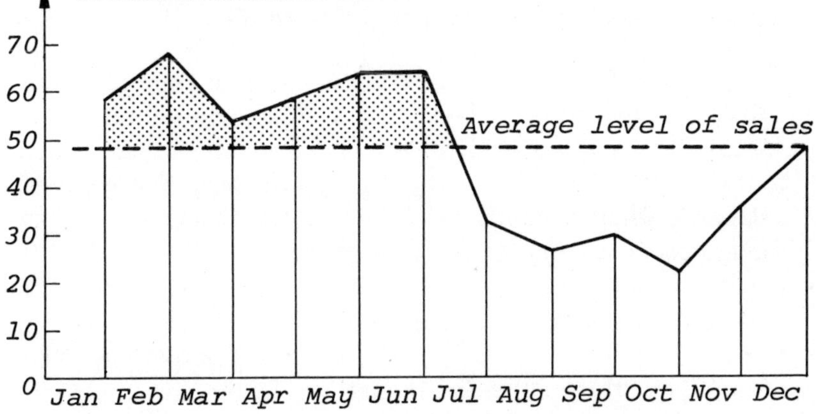

FIGURE 3. TOTAL DOMESTIC AND EXPORT SALES

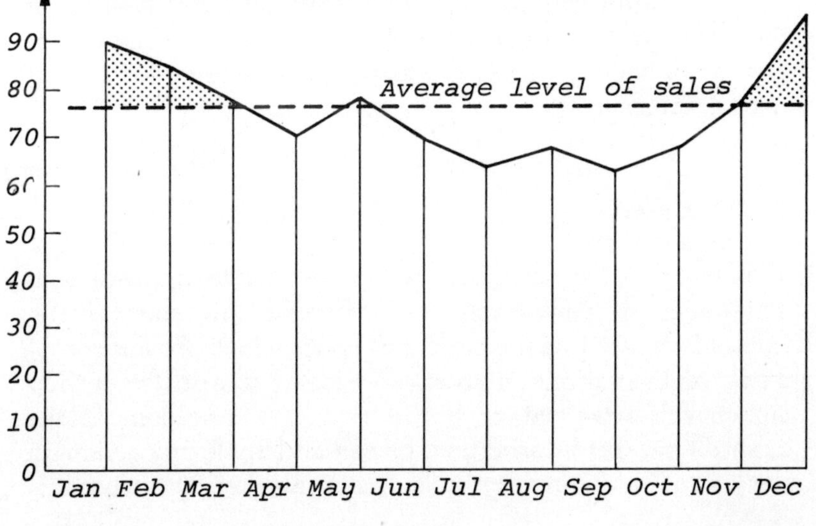

From Figure 3 (global sales — national and foreign) we can see that the variations in production are much less. The company has a more sound administration resulting from the more rational use of its manufacturing potential and of its sales team.

Of course this is only an example and many companies only realise their full turnover during a specific period. However, sales abroad can constitute a way of improving management in general.

1.1.3 A way of fighting monetary fluctuations

One of the advantages of exporting is that exchange rates are subject to considerable fluctuations. When the pound is devalued British goods, which are normally sold abroad under normal trading conditions, become particularly competitive. Likewise, when a country revalues its currency the sale of foreign goods are in a more favourable position on the British market. In the same way, when a foreign country devalues its currency its goods are easier to export and can therefore compete against national products. Some exporters take advantage of these currency fluctuations by manufacturing in pounds sterling and selling in other currencies. This exchange rate speculation can also turn to the exporter's disadvantage if the parity of the foreign currency falls. The exporting company can provide against this situation by obtaining the correct market information.

1.1.4 A marketing tool

Exporting, as we have just seen, helps you to improve your knowledge of your product with regard to your rival's, especially as regards the price. For goods which are not competitive on the national market can become competitive if their currency is devalued or if the pound is revalued. If the exporter has this information, he can anticipate any action on the part of his competitor in the British market. Therefore it is advisable for the national company to consider which price and advertising policies to choose. The data on his competitors, obtained through exporting, is not the only information available. Having entered the foreign market the exporter can become familiar with the development of the competitor's products and with the market itself. Then the exporter's technical department can begin to make the necessary improvements to its own products or develop new products suitable for the market. Innovation is one of the most important factors in a company's development and exporting is one of its principal sources.

The export salesman comes up against foreign customers as well as rival goods in the foreign markets. This rather self-evident statement is important because a Spaniard will not always react to a particular product in the same way as a German or a Japanese. Keeping in constant touch with foreign markets not only results in the creation of new products but also the discovery of new applications for these products.

1.1.5 Securing investments

Through exporting, the State can obtain the foreign currency it needs to buy goods from abroad, and particularly energy products such as oil. It is understandable that the authorities are trying to promote national exports so that this foreign currency is assured.

There are many measures taken by the State to aid exporters through organisations such as the Export Credits Guarantee Department, the British Overseas Trade Board, and the Department of Trade Commercial Relations and Export Divisions, including:

— zero VAT rating;
— help in finding agents abroad;
— information on potential customers;
— information on customs tariffs;
— statistical data on foreign markets;
— facilities for obtaining bank loans for export operations covered by the ECGD;

— purchasers' and suppliers' credits;
— payment guarantess on invoices issued abroad as part of a comprehensive insurance policy;
— financial help with trade fairs and exhibitions held abroad.

Exports are of vital necessity to the State in any economic system apart from that of autarkic protectionism. Exports are also vital for the company because they enable it to progress and it must not be forgotten that a company which does not progress, regresses.

1.2 Structure of exports

1.2.1 Which marketing method to adopt

We have not as yet discussed the export department itself because it is often difficult for the small or medium-sized concern actually to separate domestic sales from exports. Usually an export department consists of one person who is responsible for sales, and a secretary. As pointed out at the beginning of the book, it is not the company that sells but the foreign customer who buys. Then the small or medium-sized concern ventures into exporting.

Sales abroad are increasing and becoming more and more complex because of customs, outstanding debts, correspondence in foreign languages etc., and the company's managing director decides to put someone in charge of exports. An export department is born!

The newly-formed department endeavours to expand and only too often its development is haphazard and unorganised. But organisation is vital, for the development of the export department depends on it. There are various possibilities open to the company which wishes to begin exporting. One is to have one or more representatives travelling around the country trying to obtain orders. A second is to have one or more agents to distribute the goods abroad. The term 'agent' is used in its widest sense, that is, as a middleman. A third is for one small company to combine with other small concerns who manufacture similar or complementary goods. It is then possible for the small companies to open their own agency; something which is usually the province of the large company which is well-versed in the art of exporting and whose sales volume justifies such a policy.

Selecting which of these marketing methods to adopt depends on many factors.

Selecting the sales area: It goes without saying that it is easier for a company to send its salesmen to Belgium than to Brazil or Japan. The question of distance must be taken into account. A visit to Brazil or Japan represents an investment twenty times higher than that of a visit to Belgium or the Netherlands. It is certainly difficult to make such a visit pay. Of course this is not the sole criterion, or exporting would be totally out of the question as a ticket on the underground works out cheaper than an aeroplane ticket.

The language problem is of prime importance: Although it is usually possible to carry out business abroad in English it is nevertheless better to negotiate in the language of the country concerned. It is possible to group together a number of countries with the same language and to entrust the whole area to one salesman who can speak that language.

Selecting the product: The more technical a product, the more difficult it is to find people capable of selling it. It also becomes more difficult to market it without having recourse to specialist agents who may also market rival ranges. Which decision to take also depends on the intrinsic value of the product. For example, selling printing machines worth several thousands of pounds sterling justifies extensive travel, i.e. outside Europe. Training an actual employee of the company is always easier and more efficient than training an agent who may live several thousand kilometres away. Also, an agent who represents other companies will have neither the time nor the desire to devote himself entirely to the products produced by the company concerned. Of course there are exceptions to this rule but this depends on the particular circumstances involved.

Selecting the customer and the geographic distribution: To continue with the example used above of a company producing printing machines. If the market consists of thirty potential customers, it would seem more sensible to sell through the company's sales representatives rather than through a network of agents. However, after the first sale has been made the problem alters, as the dispatch and maintenance of the machines require the services of full-time staff, technicians etc. The next stage is appointing an agent to be responsible not only for an after-sales service but also for promoting sales.

Of course not all goods can be distributed in the same way; the apportionment of fixed and proportional costs must be carefully examined. It is particularly difficult to apply this solution when there are many customers throughout several countries and where each individual customer only has a low sales potential. Even so, like every other customer he still requires regular visits and in particular, technical assistance and an after-sales service. In this case the company's sales representative, who is travelling all over the country, cannot possibly be an economic proposition. Only an agent who has a well-organised network can efficiently market his principal's goods abroad and also follow up these sales. Setting up a subsidiary company abroad must be ruled out completely because of the high costs this would involve for the small or medium-sized concern.

The national attitudes and marketing methods of the country selected: It must be recognised that certain countries such as Japan, members of COMECON, North Korea etc. do not hold many opportunities for the lone salesman. For example, it is very difficult to establish oneself in Japan without the aid of a local agency or at least having a local agent and local retailers. COMECON countries such as the USSR, with planned economies, present other difficulties. The first problem is the 'introduction'. In fact it is often almost impossible to get to know the actual user of your product. Also, even if he is known, he is rarely the purchaser and one must therefore deal with the relevant central purchasing office. Although it is possible for large companies with important contracts to negotiate personally with the purchasing offices this is not the case with the small company. In fact, a large number of bilateral missions set up by agencies or by Chambers of Commerce not only represent a large investment but potentially they can only make themselves pay in the long- or medium-term. The only choice for the small company is to deal through a well-known accredited agent with reliable references. When all these factors have been considered, a marketing policy can be adopted.

Here are three examples of companies who are about to select their export policy.

The first is a medium-sized company, employing 100 people, which specialises in manufacturing printing machines. Thirty per cent of its turnover comes from exports. The unit price of its machines is between £100,000 and £500,000. Although it has a large turnover it sells a relatively small number of machines. After careful consideration of the different methods open to it the management chooses the following policy. It divides the world into five sectors: USA and Canada; Latin America, Spain and Portugal; Africa; Western Europe; and Eastern Europe.

As the company already exports to the USA and Canada it has an agreement with a firm which has a large stock of spare parts and can ensure an after-sales service and the continued maintenance of the machines sold.

The sales representatives who are responsible for Latin America and Western Europe must make three or four round trips in the region every year. Unlike these two regions where most of the sales are personal sales, the other regions, i.e. Africa, Asia and Eastern Europe, are handled by accredited agents and companies especially set up in those areas. Each representative must master the principal language of his territory and is entirely responsible for the area as far as marketing and administration are concerned. When this company reaches a turnover of about £2 million it may then expand by opening branches or representative offices abroad.

In a company which is gradually becoming more international by nature, an international division must gradually take the place of the export department.

The second company — which employs 50 people and has a turnover of £800,000, twenty per cent of which comes from exporting—specialises in manufacturing duplicators and office equipment. This company chooses to market its goods through a network of agents on commission, or importing agents. The agents, who are appointed by country, come from companies specialising in the distribution of office equipment. Therefore they actually buy the merchandise which they then supply direct to their customers. The agent can offer a permanent after-sales service by buying a stock of spare parts.

The third company is smaller, employing only 12 people. It has a turnover of £200,000 and manufactures parlour games. As the company cannot assume the full cost of such a small export department itself, the managing director decides to combine with some other games manufacturers to promote jointly their products abroad.

So we have three entirely different methods of marketing. The first, which involves high costs, enables the company to have tighter control over the market and to sell on a personal basis straight to the customer, thus eliminating the agent's profit margins. The second method has the advantage of not entailing heavy expenditure on the part of the company except for personnel and travel expenses

However, this method does have the disadvantage of smaller profit margins and a less familiar knowledge of the market. Small and medium-sized companies with restricted budgets usually prefer the second more flexible method. Also this method is often more suitable for an expanding export department. The third method, selected by a company which wishes to export but which does not have the resources to do so, has the advantage of distributing both the cost of the export department and all expenses incurred over several companies. However this could develop into a problem in the case of competing companies and it is thus difficult for the group to promote the sale of one manufacturer's goods to the detriment of another's in the same group. This is a problem encountered by a great many trade associations. The association of various small and medium-sized companies producing complementary goods would provide a more efficient service for the foreign purchaser. For example: several construction companies could form a group with one company specialising in wall coverings (i.e. tiles), another in floor coverings (i.e. carpeting), together with an architectural practice, a manufacturer of household articles and a joiner's company (i.e. windows, floors, frames etc.). It is then up to the group to employ the necessary personnel and to carry out the appropriate marketing, advertising and promotional campaigns as determined by all the members of the group.

There are many other solutions and it would be useless to try and give a comprehensive list. Selecting a marketing policy is based on the company's size, turnover, profit margins, budget, objectives and vitality.

1.2.2 Examples of flow diagrams for an export department

Example1: The company manufactures printing machines and its export department is organised on a geographical basis.

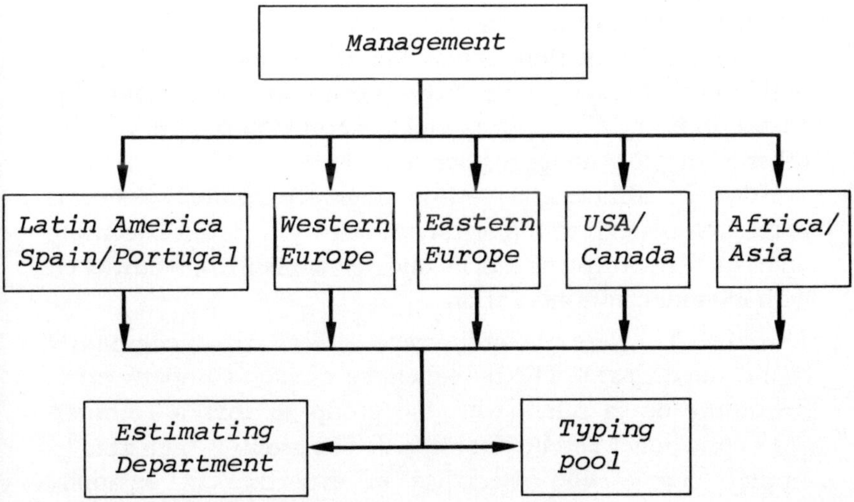

Example 2: The organisation of this export department is more complex administratively as it has a larger order book, although total orders are of a lower overall value. The head of the export department, who may have an assistant, is more than just a sales manager — he must stimulate his agents and always be looking for new openings.

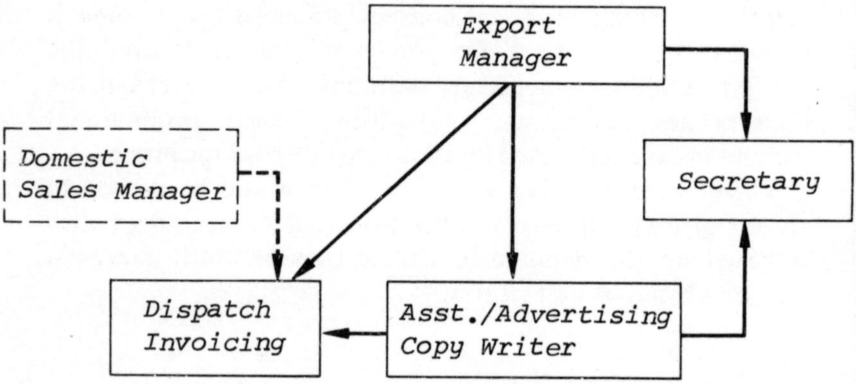

The advertising copy writer's principal task is to prepare information sheets for the agent and advertising and promotional material. In other words, he must be in constant touch with the agents or distributors abroad.

The job of the export managers' assistant or his secretary is to follow up orders, thus leaving him free to look for new sales outlets, pay regular visits to his agents and investigate his competitors' profit margins and general export policy — in other words, to manage his department.

However, although a certain degree of independence is necessary, the export department must try to avoid becoming another firm within the firm and, as a result, be burdened with too much administration.

Example 3: Here, the group replaces each small company's export department. The management of each company must constantly be in touch with the group so that a common marketing policy can be established. The group is then able to employ people who specialise in exporting in customs,

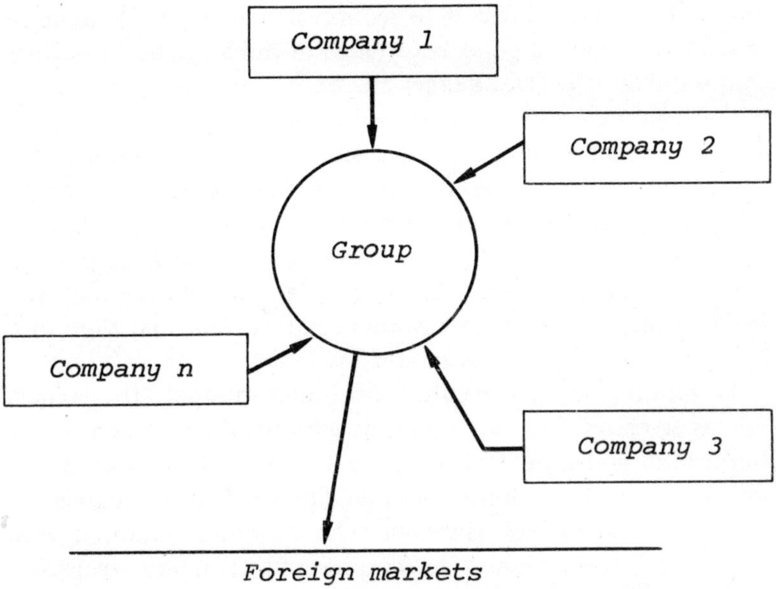

transport, specific foreign markets, linguistics etc. No small or medium-sized concern would have the resources to do this alone.

1.3 Operation of an export department

1.3.1 Personnel

The efficiency of an export department depends on its staff, whose qualifications and experience are of fundamental importance. We shall try to give a step-by-step account of how an export department is established and the role of each person in it.

The Export Manager: As his name implies the export manager is responsible for the smooth running of the department. His principal role is to secure sales abroad. To achieve this he must have a good knowledge of the area, be in perfect command of several languages and be experienced in exporting for, as we mentioned before, selling to a Japanese is totally different from selling to a Russian or a Frenchman. This means that he must be able to adapt easily and quickly to different attitudes. As an international exporter he must be very mobile as he will have to travel a great deal. Exporting means primarily selling, and just as a salesman cannot sell from his office, an exporter cannot sell from his, and therefore he must move around a good deal.

Depending on his results, aims and budget, the export manager could have an assistant who would be particularly important when he is travelling abroad. The work of the export department should not come to a halt just because the manager is away and someone who is well-acquainted with current business should be empowered to make decisions. However, the export manager should try to avoid being away too long for this could impair the smooth running of the department.

The manager must always bear in mind the department's profitability. This will be dealt with in Chapter 4.

The Manager's Secretary: The export manager's secretary is much more than a mere secretary. In many cases, apart from her normal secretarial duties she will act as his assistant. As she would also be able to speak two or more languages, she would deal with correspondence, answer the telephone, give estimates, or prepare them if there is already an estimating department within the firm. She would be in charge of following up orders, arranging invoicing and dispatching, supervising payment and chasing customers if need be. If the company sells CIF (cost, insurance, freight) she could also be made responsible for dealing with the transport agents; in other words, she would be responsible for orders in general from beginning to end.

As she is responsible for all these administrative functions within the export department, she would be capable of passing on the necessary information and orders when the manager is away which, one must remember, is quite often. The secretary keeps the sales accounts and customer's card-indexes up-to-date so that it is easy for the manager to see the current sales position and to take decisions whilst being in full knowledge of the facts.

Area Managers: Where there is a well-organised export department the principal task of the area sales managers is to sell merchandise within their specific area. As they are, for the most part, on the road, they can not only investigate and visit their customers but also obtain as much information as possible on their particular markets, i.e. technical requirements, the competition, prices, market needs etc. All these factors can help the export manager to establish a 'product' policy and decide what action to take.

While they are abroad, the area managers must keep in touch with the export department, usually by telephone, and make daily reports on their visits detailing what action should be taken at headquarters. The efficiency of this network of salesmen depends on whether the secretarial section, usually in the form of a typing pool, can carry out all the necessary administrative work at headquarters, i.e. letters of acknowledgement of visits, the dispatch of tenders, proforma invoices, invitations and general correspondence. In other words, this two-way team of salesmen outside the company and the administration within the company, proves that exporting is based on teamwork and that without it, exporting is not possible.

Additional Services: As we have already mentioned, it would be dangerous for the export department to burden itself with unnecessary administration, thus slowing down the expansion of sales abroad.

Like any commercial department whose objective is to sell, the export department has to use the company's dispatch and invoicing departments. However, it must be realised that 'export' invoicing differs from 'domestic' invoicing in that there is exemption from VAT, that the invoicing currency is not automatically the pound sterling and that special instructions have to be attached to invoices for certain countries such as Brazil, Spain, the Lebanon etc. This means that the staff must have experience in exporting even if they are not actually part of the export department. The invoice clerk must always follow the instructions given by the export department. In large companies, where exporting represents a large volume of the business, the export department should have its own invoice staff so that any errors can be avoided. This also holds true for the dispatch department because shipping abroad involves the preparation of numerous documents such as way-bills, airway bills, bills of lading etc., which are not normally required when dispatching goods within Great Britain. Furthermore, shipment abroad also requires particular care because of the long distances involved and the high incidence of parcel handling (at customs, airports, embarkation points etc.). Again, the dispatch clerk must carefully follow the instructions given by the export department.

Other departments within the company, such as the accounting, estimating and manufacturing departments, should also be organised in such a way that they can work in collaboration with the export department. However, as these are not strictly within the sphere of exporting, we shall not discuss these departments here.

1.3.2 The constituents of an export department

As we mentioned above, an export department should be staffed with qualified personnel but it is also important that they have the proper means with which to carry out their functions. Here, we are mainly concerned with the following: letters, telex and telephone. These are all of prime importance to an export department but they are not always used in the most sensible manner.

Export Mail: Export mail is one factor by which the company is judged by its foreign correspondents. The quality, style and speed of dispatch of letters will create a good, average or bad impression depending on the importance attached to this means of expression by the company. Too often, the mail is distributed late in the morning and is not attended to until several days later. This is usually due to the fact that the exporter is very busy or that he is abroad. He could reduce these delays or even avoid them altogether by delegating his authority or power of signature. A simple solution to this problem is the following method of processing the mail. As soon as it is received it should be read in its entirety and then filed in a bill-book for the day when the reply needs to be written. Urgent mail should be filed in an 'urgent' file. Letters requiring consideration or special attention should be filed separately but they should be looked at every day so that they are not forgotten. An unsigned reply should not be left to the next day for signature. It should be the responsibility of the manager's secretary to ensure that the letters are posted on the same day that they are signed. When it is a question of important mail such as invoices, estimates or confirmations of orders, it would be advisable to send them by registered or express air-mail.

Many exporters use the mail to send samples abroad. This avoids lengthy travelling delays and customs difficulties. Even though the development of international business has been based on improvements in methods of transport, and particularly in the speed of transport, it could not have developed as rapidly without improvements in the speed of dispatching mail. The letter is the first visible sign of a particular company's standing. The choice of letter heading, the way in which the letter is written and the style and language used are all of prime importance when a particular effect is required. Whenever possible, the exporter should try to write his letters in the language of the letter's country of destination, or if not, in English. Proposals or requests for orders should be clear and easily understood by the foreign customer.

Some kinds of correspondence, such as direct mailing or newsletters where only the address varies, can be typed on automatic machines especially built for this purpose. Repetitive forms of correspondence, such as order confirmation and reminders can be printed in advance on headed notepaper and then personalised when required. In order to avoid too many different kinds of documents some should be printed, for example, in French and English. Below is an example of a pre-printed reminder where only the amounts and addresses must be added.

Window envelopes are useful in that time is saved by not having to type the addresses again on the envelope and because mistakes in addresses are avoided.

Example of reminder letter:

Dear Sirs,
Messieurs,

On going through our books we find that the hereunder mentioned invoices amounting to £ are still unpaid.

En revisant nos comptes nos services comptables nous avisent que certaines factures d'un montant de £ restent à ce jour impayées.

Our terms of payment are 'invoices to be paid on receipt', therefore we would appreciate your early settlement.

Nos factures étant payables à réception, nous vous prions de bien vouloir procéder au reglement de celles-ci au plus vite.

Invoice No.	dated	amounting to £
Facture no.	du	d'un montant de £

We thank you in anticipation of your early attention and we remain yours very truly.

Dans l'attente de votre prompt règlement, nous vous prions d'agréer, Messieurs, nos salutations distinguées,

The telephone and telex: The telephone ensures the form of personal contact that a letter cannot. Inquiries and data given over the telephone would never be written down in black and white. The telephone's undeniable advantage however, could turn to a disadvantage in the case of tenders and estimates, i.e. where one copy of the communication must be kept in the company's files. But the time gained by using the telephone and the ease with which it can be used means that this costly means of communication is justly preferred in many cases.

Also information could be given over the telephone and then confirmed by letter to avoid any mistakes.

The telex has a number of advantages over the letter and the telephone. It enables one to contact the foreign customer as quickly as the telephone. Also it reduces the problem of the various time lags between countries. A telephone call from London to Los Angeles at 2.0 p.m. reaches the recipient at 6.0 a.m. because of the eight-hour time lag between these two cities. This means that the exporter has to plan his international calls. Furthermore, if the proposed recipient is not in his office when the call is put through, time is wasted. However, a telex sent from London arrives on the recipient's desk at any hour of the day or night and he will receive the message at once or at least as soon as he arrives in the office. Even so, the telex does not involve the same personal contact as the telephone. As both the telex and the letter are written documents which record information they are recognised as official evidence by British and foreign legal systems in the case of litigation. Like the telephone, the telex is more expensive than a letter and is charged on the basis of time. With telexes, the time factor can be reduced by recording the message on a punched tape and this results in a lower cost. In a study of the telex, D.R. de Massy, a consultant in international trade, points out 'that a three-minute transmission by telex using a reader means that a text of 200 words, i.e. a typed page 21 cm. by 29.7 cm., can be transmitted.' As a general principle, it is better to send a message by telex because of its lower unit cost. In addition, the high percentage of dead time in telephone calls is eliminated by using the telex.

Chapter 2

Selling Abroad

2.1 Decisions to be taken before tackling a foreign market

2.1.1 Selecting a market and finances
2.1.2 Marketing strategy and its constituents
2.1.3 Marketing strategy and sales incentives

2.2 The technical aspect of exporting

2.2.1 The sales contract
2.2.2 Methods of payment and dispatch of goods

Chapter 2

2.1 Decisions to be taken before tackling a foreign market

2.1.1 Selecting a market and finances

In Chapter 1 we looked at the various marketing policies from which the exporter could choose. Once he has decided on the market, he should study those where he is going to concentrate his investigation. In order to do this effectively he must divide up the market into sectors.

This division, initially on a geographical basis, can be achieved in three stages:

1. Researching into the countries concerned. In Great Britain this is usually carried out by a specialist organisation, a prime example of which is the British Overseas Trade Board. The exporter can also obtain information from the various UK embassies.
2. A visit to the area with a view to developing contacts.
3. On his return, the exporter can then compile his sales estimates and establish his export policies on the basis of the information compiled during the second stage.

Of course, this initial division by countries is subjective, for example: Arab countries, countries in eastern Europe, French-speaking Africa, Latin America etc.

In this way the exporter makes his initial selection on the basis of his knowledge of the markets, the activities of his competitors and other contracts which have been concluded. However, these criteria are not the only ones to be taken into account, for just because a competitor has succeeded or failed in a particular market, does not necessarily mean that the exporter must make a systematic study of all the information available to him on these countries.

INTERNATIONAL TRADE ADVISORY BOARDS: A list of specialist organisations and international trade consultants can be obtained from the Export Marketing Research Adviser (1) which can research into the markets selected by the exporter.

Therefore, the exporter can choose between carrying out his market research alone or not. Whatever his decision he should be aware of the various British organisations which are at his disposal.

These organisations, which offer many possibilities to the British exporter, are dealt with clearly and fully in the British Overseas Trade Board publication *'Export Handbook'*.

THE BRITISH OVERSEAS TRADE BOARD: *Literature on international trade:* A specialist magazine called *Trade and Industry* is published every week. It deals with foreign markets, various insurance policies proposed by the ECGD, various international trade regulations, marketing methods etc.

Hints to Business Men: These booklets also give the reporter a great deal of economic and commercial information on individual foreign markets.

The Export Intelligence Service (EIS): The EIS supplies detailed information on foreign markets to British exporters for only a small charge.

It can also provide proof of identity on potential customers or agents, data on possible foreign outlets and international invitations to tender abroad, lists of foreign visitors to Great Britain and information on possible joint ventures with foreign concerns etc.

Customs Information Department: This department can supply all the relevant customs information on the exporter's products. In this way, the exporter can get to know the

(1) Export Marketing Research Adviser, Export Services and Promotions Dept., Export House, 50 Ludgate Hill, London EC4M 7HU (tel. 01-248 5757, ext. 7263) Telex 8861 43 DTI EXPORT LDN.

nomenclature used and the different customs duties and import taxes in force in various countries.

COMMERCIAL COUNSELLORS ABROAD: Once the exporter has collected all this information he must try to assess it. This can be done by contacting the commercial counsellors in British embassies abroad and sending them details of his company, its activities and his intention of investigating that particular foreign market. In particular the exporter must not forget to attach a comprehensive list of the goods that he manufactures. His letter could also give notice of any intended visits in the next few months so that the counsellor has sufficient time to enquire into the market concerned. These counsellors are also in a position to be able to give the exporter useful addresses of potential customers, possible agents etc., who could be contacted when the exporter visits that country.

At all events, any information collected by these commercial counsellors is of immense use to the exporter and should merit his close attention.

OTHER ORGANISATIONS: Other organisations such as the large banks, through their branches abroad, the Customs administration, British Chambers of Commerce abroad, professional associations etc. can provide the exporter with useful information.

EXPORT CREDITS GUARANTEE DEPARTMENT:
Selling abroad is often synonymous with payment difficulties and considerable investment resulting in the need for bank loans. The British government established the Export Credit Guarantee Department to assuage these problems and to give financial assistance to the British Exporter.
Comprehensive insurance: The exporter can cover up to 90 or 95 per cent of his exports with this type of policy. This means that invoices unpaid at the time of export are covered in the maximum amount guaranteed by the ECGD.

The exporter can therefore insure all his exports or at least a large proportion of them. He can exclude certain markets from this guarantee, provided that a balance is maintained between high and low risk markets.

Suppliers' credit: The comprehensive short-term guarantee has been designed to provide a comprehensive insurance for a volume of sales, on credit terms up to six months, at a low premium (1). The policy holder usually tries to insure all his exports for a period of at least one year.

The guarantee does not cover those goods whose invoices must be paid within this twelve months.

The maximum credit authorised by this ECGD guarantee depends primarily on the customer involved.

— For a new customer, the maximum is £250.

— For an established customer the maximum is £5,000. In this case the exporter must obtain proof of the customer's credit worthiness from a bank before this credit is granted.

— For higher amounts the authorisation of the ECGD is required.

This policy covers all risks under contract, i.e.,

1 purchaser's insolvency;
2 delays in payment;
3 production risks or the risk of the merchandise not being accepted by the purchaser, whatever the reason may be;
4 economic and administrative risks;
5 war and acts of God.

Under this policy the ECGD guarantees the exporter up to 90 per cent of the invoiced amount in the case of delays in payment or the purchaser's insolvency (1 and 2), up to 72 per cent in the case of the merchandise not being accepted by the purchaser (3) and 95 per cent in all other cases.

Any risks are naturally reduced by insurance policies which cover up to 90 or 95 per cent of the unpaid invoices. However, the small and medium-sized company's main problem lies in liquidity.

The holder of this ECGD policy can obtain a credit from his bank for up to 100 per cent of the investment required, at a low interest rate.

(1) *see the brochure on this subject published by the ECGD.*

Purchaser's credit: A British bank can grant a foreign customer a purchaser's credit to buy British goods. Of course a credit will only be granted if the sum involved is large enough to warrant this. The minimum is £1 million. Repayment can be made on a medium or long-term basis, depending on the contract and the size of the loan made by the British bank. Both capital and interest are covered up to 100 per cent by the ECGD.

The seller receives 10 – 20 per cent of the amount specified in the contract, once it has been signed and this is paid directly by means of a loan contract so that there is no risk of non-payment and there is a forceful argument that the sale has been executed.

2.1.2 Marketing strategy and its constituents

In the previous chapter we discussed how to select a marketing policy. It goes without saying that even though the organisation of the export department depends on this marketing policy, the policy itself is dependent on the market. This interdependence between the policy and the prospective market means that the marketing policy must be adjusted to suit the market selected. Is this policy suitable for the market in question? Is there a more efficient marketing method? etc.

The exporter must have answers to all these questions before he actually enters the prospective markets. Marketing policies, which we looked at briefly in the first chapter, cannot be limited just to the organisation of the export department or to the distribution method selected. Product, publicity and promotion, and price policies must also be carefully defined and made an integral part of the future marketing policy. A marketing strategy is determined by examining this marketing policy and by checking all its constituents and the balance between them, and also the funds required to put it into practise.

PRODUCT POLICY: As with all the other constituents of the marketing policy, the product policy must have already been considered when selecting a market. But a real product policy can only be defined when a foreign market has been chosen, assuming of course that the product is not incompatible with the market in question (prohibition etc). The exporter must therefore make an objective evaluation of his product and decide whether it is marketable in this foreign market.

Now we shall try to show how this evaluation of a product is carried out. The following questionnaire is only given as a guideline.

— Does the product meet the needs of the market?

— Which new applications of the product can be considered for this new market?

— Does the product offer any particular advantages for this new market?

— Is the technical performance of the product acceptable in this market? Example: an exporter who wishes to sell mechanical calculators in Japan would probably have very little success because of the electronic calculators already manufactured in Japan.

— Is the product out of date as far as this market is concerned?

— Is the product too advanced, technically, for this market? Example: At present it is very difficult to sell automatic cash dispensers to under-developed countries such as India, or some African countries.

— Is the product compatible with the country's climatic conditions? Example: it would be relatively difficult to sell air-conditioners in Scandinavia.

— Is there a way of turning disadvantages to advantages? Example: In itself, selling identity cards in countries with a high illiteracy rate seems to be an anomaly, but these printed cards could be used to record information, in particular the name of the holder. In this way, a disadvantage is turned into an advantage.

An exporter who pays a visit to an under-developed country and notices that hardly anybody wears shoes, could react in two totally different ways, depending on whether he is a pessimist or an optimist. If he is a pessimist, he will feel that there is no market for shoes in a country where everybody goes about barefoot. But if he is an optimist he will look at the country as a huge potential market because of the fact that nobody owns a pair of shoes.

— Are rival products the same as in their country of origin or have the technical performance, design or packaging been altered? Example: cigarettes are packaged differently, depending on the country involved. In Britain, France and Germany they are sold in packets of twenty. In the USA they are sold in cartons containing 10 packets and in Spain and Portugal they are sometimes sold individually. It is the same with aspirins: they are packed in bottles of 100 or 250 tablets in the USA, tubes of 25 in Europe and in booklets of 2 or 4 in Mexico. An exporter who wants to sell sugar in the USA has to export it mainly in granules and not in lump form, as the latter only represents a small part of the US sugar market.

— Does the product comply with the laws of the foreign country? Sugar lumps exported to the USA must be packaged in separate units of one, two or three lumps, under the current health laws. Likewise, an exporter selling electric motors to the USA must ensure that they are explosion-proof, etc. It is in the exporter's interest to have his product checked by the various relevant bodies in each country (standard institutes, ministries etc.) before he begins to canvas the market.

— Does the product suit the habits prevalent in the country? Once again taking the USA as an example, it would seem at first quite understandable if a manufacturer of household appliances became interested in the USA as a potential market for coffee mills, as it is a large consumer of coffee; but because of the American habit of using special powdered coffee in their percolators, it would be practically impossible to sell even the smallest coffee-mill there. However, electric percolators would be an ideal article to sell bearing in mind their habits as far as coffee is concerned.

— Is the product either manufactured or produced in large quantities, or even exported by this particular country? Example: an exporter of wooden furniture would have very little chance of breaking into the Scandinavian market. For the same reason a cotton exporter should avoid markets such as West Africa — the principal producer of cotton.

PRICE POLICY: Although the price factor is not automatically the determining factor when selling, it is still of fundamental importance. The price policy, as well as the product policy, is dependent on the position *vis-à-vis* the competitors. The quality-price ratio must be greater, on the whole, than that of the competition. The exporter must be familiar with these points in order to fix his prices.

The product's cost price : This is usually fixed on the basis of the company's turnover, but sales forecasts, i.e. production envisaged, must also be taken into account.

Costs of transportation and insurance : The exporter should consult various transport companies in the country where the sales campaign is to be carried out, and find out their charges for transportation and insurance for all methods of transport which may be used (road, air, sea) in terms of the tonnage likely to be transported.

In the case of transportation by air, the exporter must find out whether his products can benefit from favourable tariffs or co-rates. In order to do this, he must know his product's position on the IATA (International Air Transport Association) listings. Co-rates applicable for certain destinations, are based on a minimum weight. It will sometimes be to the advantage of the exporter to declare his merchandise at an artifically high weight in order to benefit from these preferential tariffs. This is a perfectly legal procedure.

Various import taxes and customs duties : When the exporter has calculated the price of his product in the particular country in question, he can draw up a table of selling prices FOB and CIF (customs paid) by applying the relevant profit margin factors. In this way he can find out whether his product is competitive on arrival in the foreign country after taking into account the different taxes and customs duties he may be subject to in different countries, the various means of transport used and commissions taken. Then he can investigate whether customs duties imposed on his products vary depending on the exporting country. For example, in Commonwealth countries, the same product is subject to different customs duties, depending on from where it is dispatched and in which country it originated. A French product exported to Australia will be more heavily taxed than a product from Great Britain. In the same way, a product exported to Germany will benefit from preferential rates if it comes from another Common Market country.

The exporter is in a better position to evaluate his position *vis-à-vis* his competitors' products and can calculate the advantages and disadvantages of different prices in exporting to a particular country when he is in full possession of the facts as far as transport costs and customs charges are concerned.

Agents' commissions: If the merchandise is being distributed by an agent, the exporter must know what commission he charges, so that he can compare the final sale price of his product to that of his competitors. An agent acting in the name of the exporting company is usually paid in the form of a comission. As the exporter is usually responsible for invoicing it is easy to check the agent's commission charges. However, in the case of an importing agent who acts in his own name, or in the name of his company, on behalf of a principal, it is sometimes difficult to establish the actual size of his commission. In this case it is up to the exporter in his negotiations with the agent, to fix the rate of commission and to ask to be informed of the agent's proposed selling prices. The importing agent's commission is usually calculated on the CIF price (customs paid). This means charging commission on transportation, insurance, customs duties etc . . . . In the case of a commission agent, the exporter calculates the commission on the FOB price. The commission agent's rate of commission will naturally be lower than the importing agent's rate of commission because the cost of outstandinf debts, risks of non-payment etc, are, in this case, the responsibility of the exporter. It is therefore advisable to fix a reasonable rate of commission with the agent based on the amount of work demanded of him.

When the pattern of 'customers' selling prices is established it is easy to compare them with the competitors' prices. Also, an export price policy can be established by using and updating this pattern of prices. The marketing strategy, as far as prices are concerned, means studying the influence of price increases and decreases on the turnover and on the profit margins.

For example, a price increase can result in a sharp fall in the turnover but not a decrease in the gross profit margins. It could result in an increase in the gross profit margin. In the same way, a price decrease can sometimes reduce the gross profit margin whilst increasing the turnover.
Example: The FOB sales price is 100. Transport costs and customs duties = 65. The agent's commission = 55 per cent on the FOB price. The sale price = 225. The number of articles sold is 100. The unit cost price = 60. The company's turnover = 10,000, the profit margin is 40 per cent, i.e. a gross profit margin of 4,000. The global market distribution, as regards the price of articles of a similar quality is as follows:

Share of the market	20%	65%	15%

P = 180 P = 210

The majority of sales are at a lower price between 180 and 210. If the exporter decides to lower his prices by 10 per cent he will set his FOB sale price at 90 instead of 100. The final sale price is therefore set as follows:

FOB selling price	=90
Transport and insurance	=10
Customs duties (50%)	=50
Agent's commission (55%)	=50
i.e. a selling price to the customer of	200

Therefore, the exporter must sell more articles at this lower price to reach the same turnover. The number of articles which must be sold is therefore 10000/90 = 112. However, to retain the same gross profit margin he must sell 4000/30 = 134. The exporter must answer the following questions:
— Is it possible to sell at least 34 more articles by lowering the selling price by 10 per cent?

— What extra share of the market could be obtained by lowering the process by yet another 10 per cent?
— What should the selling price be to obtain a turnover with the optimum gross profit margin?

These same questions should also be asked when the prices are increased: What will be the effect on the turnover and the profit margins?

Once this price policy has been established it must be incorporated into, and adapted to, the export marketing policy.

PUBLICITY AND PROMOTIONAL POLICY: The third constituent of a marketing policy is the publicity and promotional policy; an element which requires the exporter's full attention. Just as with the product and price policies, it is closely linked to, and dependent on, the marketing policy.

The policy will differ according to the marketing method used, i.e. whether the exporter sells directly or through branches or agents abroad. It will also differ according to the product concerned. The matter becomes even more complex when one takes into consideration that the exporter will always be dealing with an international clientele, which is not only different in nature but which also embodies very different attitudes.

The exporter will choose between different kinds of advertising methods and media depending on the nature of his product.

Trade fairs and exhibitions : Trade fairs and exhibitions, which are often used by exporters, are the principal method of sales promotion abroad. By exhibiting his goods at a fair abroad, whether it is a trade fair or not, the exporter can publicise his goods, evaluate the state of the market, see potential agents etc . . . . and above all institute future sales. Although the actual presence of the exporter is important at trade fairs and exhibitions in W. Europe, it is even more important in countries with planned economies such as the USSR, E. Europe and China, where there is no other way for the exporter to contact his potential customers personally. The fact that the BOTB has a department which specialises in trade fairs and exhibitions shows how important they are in promoting British goods abroad. Every year the Department of Trade and Industry publishes a list of specialist trade fairs and exhibitions abroad. British exhibitions abroad are also organised on a regular basis by various national organisations. Of course, an exporter cannot automatically participate in every exhibition abroad. There must be a selection process and usually the exporter will only take part in exhibitions held in countries where he is canvassing for business.

Naturally, the process of taking part in an exhibition abroad depends on the marketing methods he uses. If the exporter deals through importing agents it is up to them to exhibit the exporter's products in their name. In this way, the exporter's financial participation depends on the type of agreement concluded with the agent, but on the whole it is the agent who assumes the entire financial burden of organising the exhibition. In the case of a commission agent, i.e. where he is selling in the name of his principal, or where the selling is direct, the exporter is responsible for organising the exhibition of his goods and is liable for all the expenses incurred in doing so. In this case, the agent only has to furnish physical and moral assistance before and during the exhibition.

Of course, organising an exhibition abroad is much more complicated than organising one on the national territory. The exporter must dispatch his goods, samples, literature, and spare parts. There are a great many customs and administrative formalities to be completed as the goods exhibited may either be sold or sent back to the exporting country. In addition, the exporter must be prepared for all eventualities as, due to the fact that he could be several thousand kilometres away, there can be no question of him returning to his headquarters to pick up anything that may be missing. (See Appendix 2 for an example of a 'trade fair contract' for an exhibition in the USSR.) Trade fairs and exhibitions abroad are one of the principal ways for the exporter to penetrate foreign markets.

Conferences : The exporter could organise conferences to publicise his products abroad, to achieve the same results as participating in trade fairs and exhibitions. Conferences are also particularly effective in countries with planned economies. The exporter can exhibit his goods at a conference as long as they are not too bulky. Or, as is more generally the case, he can use audio-visual equipment, films and transparencies as a way of presenting his company's goods. One advantage of audio-visual equipment is being able to record information in the language spoken by the audience in question. The choice of material depends not only on one's budget, but also on the size of the audience. If there is a small audience, the exporter can use equipment like video-tape cassettes so that he can travel easily with all his equipment. There is a great variety of equipment available thanks to developments in modern technology.

Direct mailing: Direct mailing is widely used when selling by post and is a way of reaching a large number of potential customers at a reasonable cost. Direct mailing is very useful when selling products which do not need any technical demonstration to a particular group of customers. Before deciding on a campaign of direct mailing, the exporter must examine its estimated profitability. It is possible to calculate this by using s statistical base of 4 to 7 per cent of the replies recieved and about 2 per cent of the orders received; this percentage can vary according to the nature of the product involved.

Advertising in the media: One can put advertisements in both foreign and British specialist magazines. In Chapter 3 we shall discuss how an exporter can motivate his agents and take an active part in foreign advertising campaigns.

Literature: Any literature used by the exporter can also be considered as an important method of advertising. Unlike any literature used domestically, export literature must be prepared in several different languages. The exporter has the choice of either preparing it in several different languages or producing a different set of literature in each language. In this case the question of cost is the deciding factor.

The trade mark: Although the trade mark cannot be considered as an integral part of the advertising policy, it is still an important factor which merits the exporter's full attention. It must be tested abroad before any advertising or promotional campaign is undertaken. For example, the same product could be sold under different trade marks in different countries. A Japanese company trying to sell hunting rifles under the trade mark 'MIROKU' will not be very successful until it changes this trade mark. It is therefore most important for the exporter to enquire about the significance of that particular trade mark in the country concerned; what it could evoke there and whether it can be pronounced easily or is difficult to remember. The actual advertising methods used depend on the advertising and promotional policy selected: advertisements, direct mailing, literature, exhibitions etc., together with the overall publicity and promotional budget available. The budget is fixed not only in relation to the size of the existing turnover, but also to the estimated turnover.

Advertising and promotional strategy lies in distributing funds between the products, countries and agents as objectively as possible.

One solution is to halve the budget. One half for internal expenses such as expenditure on trade fairs in Britain, direct mailing throughout the world and literature, and the other half for external expenses with regard to a particular country, agent or campaign, e.g. taking part in a trade fair in Germany, putting advertisements in a magazine in Italy, financial help given to agents etc.

A logical way of dividing the budget, based on the sole criterion of profitability, can be achieved by compiling a table of sales and sales forecasts by country.

INTERPRETATION OF THE TABLE (ON PAGE 39) ON THE DIVISION OF AN ADVERTISING BUDGET.

Column 1 : 1973 turnover
Column 2 : Investment in advertising in 1973
Column 3 : 1974 turnover
Column 4 : Investment in advertising in 1974
Column 5 : Returns for 1974. This is calculated by the ratio between the 1973 and 1974 turnovers and the investment in advertising for 1973 and 1974.

Table showing the division of an advertising budget

COUNTRIES	Col. 1 1973 turnover	Col. 2 Invest-ment on advert-ising	Col. 3 1974 turnover	Col. 4 Invest-ment on advert-ising	Col. 5 Returns	Col. 6 Multiply-ing factor	Col. 7 Forecast 1975 turnover	Col. 8 Forecast expendi-ture on advert-ising	Col. 9 Max budget	Col. 10 Budget
Germany	1 200	24	1 500	60	32	0.96	3 000	90	86.5	75.5
South Africa	300	6	350	10	40	1.2	1 400	42	50.5	44
Belgium	500	28	1 500	40	29.4	0.88	3 500	105	92	80.3
Spain	600	24	800	38	22.5	0.67	1 600	48	32	28
U.S.A.	800	12	1 800	60	36.1	1.08	3 000	90	97	84.7
France	2 400	12	3 100	55	82	2.46	4 200	126	310	270.6
Netherlands	700	33	1 700	40	32.8	0.98	2 900	87	85	74.2
Italy	1 000	40	1 500	70	22.7	0.68	2 700	81	55	48
Portugal	200	12	300	18	16.7	0.50	450	13.5	7	6.1
Scandinavia	300	16	380	32	14.2	0.43	550	16.5	7	6.1
Switzerland	200	13	300	17	16.7	0.50	380	11.4	6	5.2
U.S.S.R.	1 800	80	4 770	100	36.5	1.09	8 320	249.6	272	273.3
TOTAL	10,000	300	18,000	540	33.33	1.00	32,000	960.0	1,100.0	960.0

Column 6 : Multiplying factor of the investment in advertising. This is obtained by dividing the return for each country by the average return (33.3 per cent in our example). This factor is then applied to the forecast expenditure on advertising.
Column 7 : Forecast turnover for 1975
Column 8 : Forecast expenditure on advertising in relation to the turnover and on the basis of 3 per cent of the total estimated turnover, i.e. 960.
Column 9 : Maximum advertising budget. This is obtained by multiplying the product of the forecast expenditure on advertising (*Col. 8*) by the multiplying factor of the return (*Col. 6*).
Column 10 : Advertising budget for 1975. Then one only has to bring the advertising budget for each country (*Col. 9*) in line with the actual budget, on a proportional basis. In this example, one must multiply each budget in *Col. 9* by 0.873, given that the maximum budget is 12.7 per cent higher than the actual budget allocated, i.e. 960.

2.1.3 Marketing strategy and sales incentives

We know that the exporting company's success depends largely on its marketing strategy. Of course the measure of its success depends on how conscious the exporter is of the fact that sale incentives abroad are not automatically the same as in Great Britain. By classifying these incentives for the country where business is envisaged, the exporter is better able to gauge the balance of his various policies and as a result to achieve a marketing strategy which is really suitable for that particular market.

The exporter must define these incentives before actually beginning to categorise them. They may include the quality of the product, the after-sales service, the delivery times, prices, the currency in which payment is to be made, political relations between the various countries and introduction of the salesman.

It is certainly not very difficult to sell a modern, up-to-date product in the USA. Quality of service is of prime importance and the American or German entrepreneur will only buy the merchandise if he is sure that it will be easy for him to obtain spare parts and a good after-sales service. However, the incentives used by the salesman will differ, depending on whether he is dealing with an American or a Russian. Whilst sales are organised or 'planned', as the term suggests, in countries with planned economies, selling in capitalist countries very much depends on the ability of the salesman.

When a salesman is selling in a country with a planned economy, he should ask himself the following questions:

— Are sufficient quantities of the product already manufactured by the country in question, or even a sister country (e.g. Comecon countries)?
— Is this kind of product subject to planned purchasing?
— Is there a real need for the product in the country and is this need acknowledged by the customers?
— If the product is not 'planned', could the exporter initiate this?
— Who will buy it?

However, in the case of a capitalist country, the salesman must try to find out whether the customer wants to buy the product and above all, *when* he wants to buy it. In this case, the motivation is of a personal nature: the prestige that the purchaser can derive from the particular product that he is buying, his desire to be a leader in this field and to have a really new product, and above all, the profit which he could obtain by buying this particular industrial product. In developing countries, the financial assistance provided by the foreign governments in the form of direct or indirect loans (purchaser's credit etc.) and the terms of payment are of vital importance when selecting a supplier.

In countries in Eastern Europe the seller is sometimes forced to accept the partial or total purchase of the factory's production instead of payment. He must often accept these compensation agreements for at least a part of the final sales price. Therefore, because of the lack of convertible currencies in some Eastern European countries, the method of payment is of immense importance.

— Does the buyer's country have sufficient foreign currency to pay for its purchases?

Although it is very difficult to classify these incentives by country, we have tried to classify the most important ones for developed countries, developing countries and countries with planned economies.

Incentives in developed countries

1 Quality of the product
2 Price
3 Service

Incentives in developing countries

1 Political criteria
2 Introduction of the salesman
3 Payment of commissions
4 Terms of payment
5 Price
6 Quality
7 Delivery times

Incentives in countries with planned economies

1 Quality
2 Terms of payment
3 Price

2.2 The technical aspect of exporting

2.2.1 The sales contract

The sales contract is a contract linking the buyer and the seller. Even when reduced to its most simple form, i.e. the letter, telex etc., it is just as much of a reciprocal obligation between the two parties. The nature of the sales contract will differ according to the nature of the material sold. Nevertheless, if the exporter attends to all the factors which are common to all sales abroad, he should be able to avoid any litigation at a later date.

When the contract comes into force: A sale is concluded when both the article and the price are agreed. If he wishes, the exporter will be able to state on the contract that it will not come into effect until a deposit has been received or until the purchaser has opened a documentary letter of credit.

Description of the goods: The article and the price are the basic elements of the sales contract. The merchandise must therefore have not only a reference number but must also be fully described. The price stated in the contract is always dependent on terms of delivery and payment (see below). The exporter must also pay close attention to the invoice currency when negotiating the contract. Selling in pounds sterling is without doubt one of the surest ways of avoiding exchange losses. However, some customers wish to buy goods in their own currency for this same reason. The rate of exchange applied is that of the day when payment is made and not that of the day when the order is made. The exporter who cannot sell in pounds sterling has two alternatives if he wants to avoid the risk of losing on the exchange rate. The first is to use a stable currency. The second is to negotiate with his banker for a credit purchase in the foreign currency corresponding to the amount to be paid in the invoice currency.

Transfer of ownership: When does the buyer become the owner of the merchandise? This question, which is often omitted in international sales contracts, could give rise to many problems should legal action take place at a later date, because of the many differences between various foreign legal systems. Although in French law, 'the purchaser becomes the owner of the article sold at once, with the consent of both parties, and before it is physically transferred to him', in German law, the transfer of ownership takes place when the customer receives the merchandise. However in French law, the direct transfer of ownership at the time of order, is only valid where the goods have already been manufactured.

According to English law, transfer of ownership occurs after a Bill of Lading has been submitted to the purchaser and payment made in accordance with a Letter of Credit.

However, in the case of one or other of the parties becoming bankrupt, the legal regulations will differ according to the legal system concerned. The exporter should, therefore, include in the contract, a clause concerning the transfer of ownership and the retention of ownership, which gives him the right to regain possession of the goods in the case of partial or total non-payment. This is particularly important in the case of bankruptcy on the part of the purchaser.

Termination of the contract : As Michel Beck righly points out in a recent article in MOCI *(Moniteur du Commerce International,* the French equivalent of *Trade and Industry),* 'The size of the deposit should be large enough to dissuade the buyer from terminating the contract during the production period'. However, particularly in the case of goods which have to be manufactured especially, the exporter incurs a considerable risk. In order to ease this problem he may insert a termination clause as follows: in the case of termination of the contract on the part of the purchaser, the purchaser must pay the seller, with the agreement of the latter and on receipt of an invoice, all the expenses incurred by the seller (expenditure on research, raw materials, installation, etc.). Moreover, the purchaser must pay the seller 20 per cent of the amount still to be paid in compensation for this termination of contract. Another solution is to take out a comprehensive insurance with the ECGD. Where the contract is suspended or where the merchandise is refused on delivery, the ECGD will reimburse to the exporter any loss incurred in proportion to the sum guaranteed (72 per cent).

Delivery: Whenever possible, the exporter will state the delivery times solely as a guide; failure to observe these delivery times can in no case be binding on the seller. Where such a clause is rejected by the purchaser, which is usually the case, the dates shall, as far as possible, be given 'ex-works'. In this way any risks involved in transportation and customs clearance are avoided. The exporter should also be entirely

freed from any liability with regard to delivery dates:
— in the case of the purchaser's failure to observe the terms of payment;
— in the case where additional information, to be supplied by the purchaser, is not received by the seller within the period specified;
— in the case of a subsequent request on the part of the purchaser for modifications to be made to the merchandise;
— in the case of Acts of God (strike, lock-out, fire, flood, breakdown of machinery, disruption of work etc . . .).

Packaging: Usually, in international commerce, the merchandise sold is always considered as being packaged. However, if packaging is not included in the selling price, this must be stated in the contract. This is usually the case where the merchandise needs additional packaging for shipment by sea, which is very costly.

Guarantees: A guarantee is given for a particular period of time, determined by the nature of the goods. In the case of industrial machinery, the guarantee is often accompanied by a technical assistance contract. In this case, the exporter must pay careful attention to the conditions by which the guarantee is made. Example: the seller's guarantee, valid for a period of one year from the date of the goods' dispatch, is only applicable where the use of the material in question does not exceed 40 hours a week.

Delivery clauses: Every sales contract, should include the terms of delivery. In 1936 the International Chamber of Commerce published the rules and practices of international commerce. These rules, knowns as INCOTERMS, govern the terms of sales and in particular, of delivery, in international commerce. The responsibilities and obligations of the seller and the purchaser are specified in all cases. These INCOTERMS, revised in 1953, cover a great many points; below are the four which are most used.

EX-WORKS SALES: All expenses incurred in the seller's factory before receipt of the merchandise by the purchaser are the responsibility of the former, except where stipulated to the contrary in the contract, e.g. packaging not included. The seller's responsibility ends when the purchaser accepts the goods.

FOB (Free on board): This term, which was originally applied to consignments transported by sea, is now a general term for all forms of transport. The term FOB must always be followed by the name of the port of embarkation, the city of departure etc. e.g. FOB London for sea consignment and FOB London Airport for air consignment.

The expenses to be paid by the seller include all those incurred before the merchandise is loaded. Other similar terms are used in the case of dispatch by rail (FOR-free on rail) or by road (FOT-free on truck) etc. However, the most common term is still FOB whatever the form of transport used. The responsiblity of the exporter ends when the merchandise is loaded at the agreed place.

C & F SALES (Cost and freight) : As in the case of FOB sales, the place of delivery must be shown after the initials C & F, e.g. C & F Sydney. All expenses up to the place of delivery, with the exception of insurance, are the responsibility of the exporter.

CIF SALES (Cost insurance freight) : CIF sales are the same as C & F sales, except for insurance, which in this case is the responsibility of the exporter. This type of sale is ideal for the purchaser. CIF is always considered as customs duties not paid unless specified to the contrary, e.g. CIF New York (Customs Paid).

Terms of payment : Is payment made in cash or on credit? Is there a deposit? or a guarantee clause? What guarantees would the exporter obtain to ensure payment for his merchandies? Although a guarantee clause, often included in contracts, obliges the purchaser to pay the entire amount specified on the order, the exporter should still carefully consider the method of payment he wishes to be used. Below are the main methods of payment used in international commerce.

As we have just mentioned, the seller should normally ask for a deposit when the order is placed, not only to commit the buyer, but also to alleviate the burden on his financial resources. Whether dealing with cash or credit, the balance is one of the exporter's main worries; will it be paid?

INVOICE PAYMENTS: Whether payment is made in cash or on credit (30, 60 or 90 days), the risk of non-payment incurred by the exporter is very great. This method of payment should therefore be avoided except in the case of very good customers or agents who have had dealings with the company for many years.

PAYMENT AGAINST DOCUMENTS: Unlike the first method, cash payment against documents ensures that the exporter is paid for the merchandise as soon as it is received by the customer. In the case of a deferred payment the purchaser pays in the form of a fixed term bill of exchange. Guaranteed payment of these bills of exchange will only be effective if they are accepted by the exporter's banker. In fact, payment by unaccepted bills of exchange becomes a simple credit payment with no other guarantee than the purchaser's good faith. These bills are only an acknowledgement of the purchaser's indebtedness to the seller and will only be paid if the purchaser's bank account has sufficient funds on the day payment falls due. Acceptance of these bills by the exporter's banker prior to exporting is an assurance that these bills will be honoured.

DOCUMENTARY LETTER OF CREDIT: A documentary letter of credit, as its name suggests, combines payment against documents with the idea of export credit. The guarantees offered by this method of payment, both for the exporter and the importer., as well as the fact that the purchaser only pays when the material is received, makes this the best method of payment in international commerce. As these two methods of payment are closely linked with methods of dispatch we shall now look at the various forms of dispatch of goods.

2.2.2 Methods of payment and dispatch of goods

The exporter who wants to be paid for his merchandise should concern himself with the terms of payment well before the goods are dispatched. Payment for exports is conditioned by the way in which the goods are dispatched and the documents are transferred.

Documents : There are various types of documents which serve as a basis for payment for goods: trading documents, transport documents, customs and banking documents . . .

Commercial documents: these include invoices (proforma and final), bills of sale, certificates of origin and quality, consular invoices etc. However, the invoice is the principal document which specifies the nature and price of the merchandise to be exported.

Transport documents: both these documents and the insurance certificates vary according to the means of transport used.

MEANS OF TRANSPORT	TRANSPORT DOCUMENT
Air	Airway bill
Road	Way bill
Sea	Bill of lading
Waterways	Waterways bill of lading
Rail	Railway bill

Some of these transport documents, such as the maritime bill of lading, are negotiable (unlike the way bill which is not). These transport documents prove that the goods have been loaded, and that the exporter has indeed dispatched the merchandise. Responsibility is therefore transferred from the exporter to the forwarding agent: the captain is responsible for the merchandise in his charge. This is an acknowledgement of indebtedness, and this acknowledgement is called a bill of lading. When the merchandise is loaded, the forwarding agent can sometimes issue reservations with regard to the condition of the products in his charge. If the merchandise is acknowledged as being in good condition by the forwarding agent, the endorsement 'Clean on board' or

'Franco de Reserves' is then attached to the bill of lading. The bill of lading is therefore more easily negotiable.

Exporting using payment against documents : When the merchandise is dispatched, there are two ways open to the exporter to ensure payment for his merchandise. The first is to deliver both the merchandise and a set of the original invoices to the forwarding agent. At the same time he should dispatch a set of invoices to his customer and notify him when the merchandise is dispatched. On its arrival the forwarding agent delivers the merchandise to the purchaser on receipt of payment (where payment is to be in cash). In the case of a deferred payment, he should deliver the merchandise when the exporter's drafts have been signed. The second solution is to dispatch the merchandise through a forwarding agent and to give the banker the relevant papers (dispatch documents, customs declarations, invoices, drafts, etc.). The exporter's banker then sends these documents to his correspondent or even to the purchaser's banker. When he receives the draft he must notify his client who takes receipt of the goods on receipt of payment or signature of the drafts. When the purchaser has these documents he can take delivery of the merchandise and return the documents to the forwarding agent.

Exporting using payment against documentary letters of credit : In the case of documentary letters of credit, it is up to the purchaser to ask his banker to open a documentary credit (see Figure No. 1). The exporter must first send him a set of proforma invoices which cpecify the nature and price of the goods which are the subject of the credit.

The purchaser's banker then opens an irrevocable credit (2). In other words the purchaser's banker undertakes to pay the exporter the amount specified on the final invoice rather than the amount on the proforma invoice, on receipt of the bill of lading. A revocable credit amounts quite simply to a dispatch made against receipt of documents.

A documentary letter of credit is opened by the purchaser's banker on the instructions of the purchaser himself for a particular product, amount and length of time. This letter opening a documentary credit is then sent to the exporter's banker (2) who acknowledges receipt of the credit and notifies his client, the exporter (3). He can sometimes confirm this credit, i.e. he in turn promises to settle the exporter's debts if the purchaser's banker fails to pay. The documentary credit is then said to be irrevocable and confirmed.

The exporter can then dispatch the merchandise through his forwarding agent (4) who conveys it to its destination (5). Once the exporter is in possession of all the necessary papers (invoices, dispatch documents, insurance policy, certificate of origin etc.) he can then draw a bill on his customer which he endorses, together with the bill of lading and the insurance policy, in the name of his banker. All these documents make up the documentary letter of credit which the exporter then passes on to his banker (6). The exporter's banker accepts the documentary bill which he can discount should the client so wish (7). The exporter's banker sends the documentary bill to the purchaser's banker (the issuing bank of the documentary letter of credit) (8). The purchaser's banker can buy this bill from his client (9). The purchaser can then pass this documentary bill on to the forwarding agent so that he can take possession of his merchandise (10).

DIAGRAM OF HOW A DOCUMENTARY LETTER OF CREDIT OPERATES

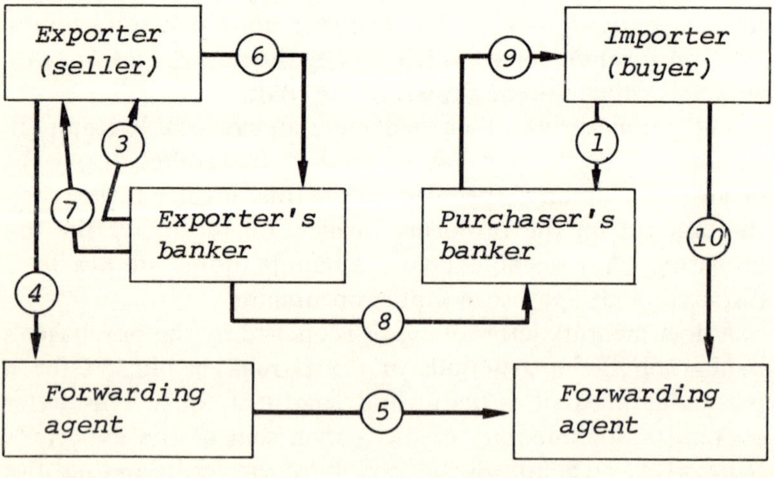

Chapter 3

Selling Abroad Through a Network of Agents

3.1 The agent

3.1.1 Why select an overseas agent?
3.1.2 The type of agent

3.2 How to find and select an agent

3.3 The contract

3.4 Visiting an agent

3.5 Motivating the agent

Chapter 3

3.1 The agent

3.1.1 Why select an overseas agent?

As we have already noted in Chapter 1, the exporter who has already selected his marketing policy can sometimes be induced to market his products through a network of agents. The exporter may decide to opt for using agents after careful consideration of the following points:

the company's turnover
export budget
structure of the export department
nature of the products to be sold
geographical distribution of the customers
countries to be investigated etc . . . .

The first three factors are indissociable for, the smaller the company's turnover, the smaller the export budget, and in consequence the structure of the export department cannot be based on a system of direct selling and even less on a system of branches abroad. The only possible solution is to use an agent as a middleman.

As we have already stated, the three other factors show that the more technically sophisticated the products, the further away are the countries to be investigated and in particular, the wider the geographic distribution of the existing and prospective customers, the more concerned the company should be to have a local base. Apart from actually having a branch in the country concerned, only an agent is in a position to deal with stocks, an after-sales service, regular investigatory visits etc.

Therefore an agent appointed for a particular country or even for a specific product, is a representative of the exporting company in the foreign country concerned. The most important factor is that the original investment will be practically nothing as far as the exporter is concerned and that as the cost of the agent is always proportional to the sales made, fixed costs are therefore ruled out.

In most cases, the company which decides to market its goods through a network of agents does not usually have large financial resources and therefore cannot make any large investments.

The fact that there are a great many agents throughout the world shows how important they are in international trade.

3.1.2 The type of agent

In their book, *Export Agents*, Colin McMillan and Sydney Paulden mention 27 different types of agents. They point out quite rightly that the very general term 'agent' covers a wide range of different trading activities. Without including the company's salaried staff who sometimes work abroad and are sometimes wrongly called 'agents', there are still a great many kinds of agents who receive their salary in the form of a commission. The agent is an intermediary between the purchaser and the exporting company, and is never an employee of the exporting company. Using this definition of an intermediary, there are commission agents who act in the name of their principal and importing agents who act in their own name and act as a buyer of the merchandise involved.

Agents acting in the name of their principal : These agents, whether they are individual or legal entities, are paid by commission on the sales they make. The commission agent usually has many facets to his business and reduces any possible risks by extending the range of products he deals in. Also, as he does not actually buy any merchandise he does not tie up any of his capital, does not incur any expenses and in particular never risks making a loss on unsold goods. In a way, the agent acts like a broker by acting as a link between the buyer and the seller and by giving commercial help to the latter. In addition, he often handles all the negotiations and the exporter only has to send out proforma invoices when the transaction is concluded.

The advantages of such an agent for the exporter : The prime advantage of a commission agent is that the exporter has only a few ties with his agent. Apart from the fact that the agent could make some large sales, if the market proves to be attractive, the exporting company can then act personally and may even contemplate setting up an office together with the agent himself.

The second advantage is that when the exporter knows his existing and potential customers better, he can then send invitations to order, and also invoices, direct to the customer and not to the agent.

The disadvantages of such an agent for the exporter : There are only a few advantages to this kind of agent, but there are many disadvantages. In fact, this type of agent usually contacts the exporting company when a customer asks to buy something and does not actually try to instigate sales himself by canvassing the market. Also, as these agents often represent a wide range of goods, they have very little time to devote to each product and naturally spend more time on those products which are profitable in the short-term. If the price or quality of the product proposed by the exporting company does not suit them, then they will not hesitate in knocking at the door of the competitors. The exporter is at the mercy of his agent as he has no way of controlling him. However, this is usually only the case with small and medium-sized companies where agents cannot gross a large turnover because of the kind of goods proposed. It is obvious that in the case of large contracts or large companies, these contracts alone are enough to motivate the agent and to ensure his loyalty towards the exporter.

However, once the goods are sold, the exporter is responsible not only for delivery but also for clearing them through customs. In other words, he must sell CIF (customs paid) with all the risks that this involves, unless of course he leaves this to the customer, with all the problems that this could raise.

The exporter invoices the customer directly. The risks of non-payment therefore fall to the exporter unless the agent is *bona fide*. Consequently the exporter must make sure that he does not pay his agent's commission until the customer has settled the account. In this way, the exporter has a means of putting extra pressure on the agent to guarantee payment of these invoices. A method which is much more reliable but which is also much more complicated administratively, is only to sell against confirmed and irrevocable documentary letters of credit.

This kind of agent is more common in transactions with countries with planned economies, such as the USSR, due to the requirements of their legal systems. The agent cannot have stocks of goods or canvas potential customers but must deal with centralised purchasing bureaux in the name of the products he represents, whether these belong to the exporting company or not. These agents, who usually come from the same country as the exporter, usually have good standing in the particular foreign country. Because of their wide experience in those markets, and also the fact that they sometimes deal in imports as well as exports, these agents are in a privileged position as far as the exporter is concerned. Compensation agreements are often concluded in these countries so that the exporter does not have to be paid in various kinds of merchandise. The two roles of the agent are (a) to act as a link between the buyer and the seller (the exporting company) and (b) to ensure that the exporter is paid in the foreign currency when the transaction is concluded. Depending on the various requirements and demands of the company, these agents usually receive a list of anticipated purchasers which is then passed on to the various manufacturers of this particular merchandise. At the same time these agents issue a list of goods to possible buyers provided by the exporter. In doing this some form of compensation is therefore payable to the agent by the exporter.

In some countries, such as those in the Middle East or Asia, an agent can benefit from his personal contacts when asking for his commission from the supplier (exporter). The commission can be in the form of a fixed sum determined in advance. He can secretly bring influence to bear on the sales of the exporter's goods. This type of agent, who could be an employee of the purchasing company, although exporters are not usually very keen on this, is sometimes very useful.

Also some important customers may suggest that their company takes on the agency having the sole aim of obtaining the best prices themselves. It is often in the interests of the exporter to refuse such a suggestion. In fact, a company which becomes an agency can obtain 'agent's prices', which are lower, and not try to promote the exporter's products elsewhere. In addition, it will be very difficult for the exporter to leave this agency without risking the loss of the market that it represents as a customer.

The agent can be either an individual or legal entity acting in the name of the exporting company. This is often the case with consignee agents. Selling by consignment is undoubtedly the least advantageous method of marketing as far as the exporter is concerned. Goods taken by the agent on consignment will not be paid for until they have been sold. If they are not sold, they are returned to the exporter, usually at his expense. A consignment sale has two major disadvantages. The first is that it is the exporter's money which is tied up and the second is that, as the agent has no money involved and as he can always return the goods to the exporter, he may not make any effort to sell them. Motivating the agent is much more difficult. Also once the agent has received his commission he will not concern himself with any after-sales service, as he has no stocks of spare parts, and again the exporter is liable. With the exception of goods sold in small quantities on a regular basis, the exporter should always try to avoid any consignment sales.

Agents acting in their own name or in the name of the company, on behalf of a principal : Unlike commission agents, importing agents actually buy the merchandise and then resell it to their customers. The biggest disadvantage of this type of agent is that as the agent actually owns the merchandise, he does not necessarily have to inform his principal of its final destination. Therefore, the exporter cannot part company with his agent without running the risk of losing all his customers. Another disadvantage is that one is selling at 'agent's prices', which are usually much lower than the 'customer's prices', so that the agent can still take his commission and remain competitive on the market. It is very difficult for the exporter to get to know the actual commission taken by the agent. And the agent who takes too large a commission runs the risk of losing a considerable amount of the exporter's business which he could have retained by using a commission agent. One answer to this is to ask the agent to make his affairs public. In this case the agent must send a copy of each invoice issued to his principal. This enables the principal not only to follow the development of the market prices and to control the size of the agent's commission, but also to gain some knowledge of his customers.

Importing agents, as their name implies, import foreign goods into their own countries and on the whole they buy FOB or even ex-works. Their commission is calculated on the CIF price, thus increasing the customer's price considerably.

Unlike commission agents or brokers, importing agents actually buy the merchandise, make every effort to resell it and in particular they usually limit the number of companies they represent. They usually specialise in a specific range of products and do business with a well-defined range of customers. They are responsible for selling the exporter's products and are also liable for ensuring an after-sale service to their customers. Because of this, they have a stock of spare parts and goods. As they invoice the customers themselves, it is they who run the risk of not being paid for the goods.

Importing agents make a substantial investment when taking on a new product; buying stocks, demonstration models, creating a special department, with salesmen who are themselves specialised in the new product, undertaking publicity and promotional campaigns etc. Therefore it is quite understandable if they ask for exclusive rights as agents. In exchange for this right, the exporter can ask them to commit themselves to an annual sales quote.

Whether they are sole agents or not, they do represent the best way for the exporting small or medium-sized company to penetrate a foreign market.

3.2 How to find and select an agent

As we have already established, an exporter can only begin to look for an agent when the product, market and type of agent has been established. Engaging an agent can take place at two very different times; either when looking for potential agents in general or when selecting an agent who seems to be the most suitable for marketing the products of the company and for defending its interests.

3.2.1 Looking for potential agents

At trade fairs and exhibitions: The exporter can set up a file on all the potential agents he has found, in the relatively recent past, at specialist trade fairs, exhibitions, salons etc. In fact, a great many foreign agents, and in particular, importing agents, offer their services at these events.

It is not a good idea for the exporter to engage someone at once without carefully considering all the potential candidates in this field. Many exporters engage their agents this way (usually for more remote countries), for the sole reason that they do not know of anyone else. They prefer to have an agent who will make some sales, however few. Although the exporter may choose, by the merest chance, the ideal agent, it still remains true that he may in this way be deviating from his main exporting policy, and may disperse his efforts and financial resources in countries where operations had not been anticipated. Furthermore, as the exporter cannot give any real help to his agent through fear of dissipating his efforts he will only obtain mediocre or even no results from his agent. It must be emphasised that a bad agent is the worst kind of publicity and that, whatever the qualities of the product, his sales opportunities would be endangered for some time to come.

Through the press: It is always possible to obtain a list of potential agents by an advertisement giving a short account of the company and its products. This advertisement may be inserted in trade magazines in the country where an agent is being sought.

Through the BOTB and commercial counsellors : As we mentioned at the beginning of Chapter 2,. the exporter can call on the BOTB's trade information services. Armed with a substantial amount of literature and above all, many years of experience of foreign markets, the BOTB can often supply the exporter with valuable information in his search for an agent, even if it cannot provide him with an exhaustive list. The exporter can also contact the commercial counsellor at the British embassy in the country concerned. He must send the counsellor a complete dossier on his company, its products and the kind of agent he is looking for. He could even meet the counsellor in person.

For a small sum the exporter can also take out a subscription to articles published by the Export Intelligence Service of the BOTB. The exporting company must specify its field of activities and specialities — electronics, food products etc. Information on their products will be sent to them every day. It costs £30 for about 150 articles. These sheets give data on the state of the markets, variations in customs duties, potential customers and agents, dates of visits by commercial counsellors normally based abroad, trade fairs and exhibitions to be held abroad etc.

Through trade associations : The exporter can make the same request to trade associations. As their name suggests they have a thorough knowledge of those companies capable of effectively representing the exporting company and can supply a detailed list of the same.

Other methods : The various methods of finding agents listed above is not exhaustive. The exporter can also make inquiries at local banks, the large British banks and their branches abroad, and in particular, British Chambers of Commerce abroad and foreign Chambers of Commerce in Great Britain.

When the exporter has the most comprehensive list possible of companies which could import his products, he must get in touch with them all by letter. He should attach to this letter any general information, if possible in the language of the country concerned, and a detailed questionnaire. This questionnaire should help the exporter to get a very clear picture of the prospective companies which could act as his agents.

Example of a questionnaire to be sent to prospective agencies

— Name of the company
— Date of foundation
— Registered capital
— Field of activities
— Names of directors
— Annual turnover
— Number of employees
— Administrative buildings: head office, branches, shops, warehouses etc.
— Does it have any shareholdings in other companies? Which companies? Extent of shareholdings.
— What kind of goods does it produce?
— Which products are represented by the company?
— What is the percentage of products imported or represented in relation to the company's turnover?
— Which are the companies already represented?
— Their addresses
— Are they represented on an exclusive basis or not?
— What is the legal nature of the agency?
— Is the company *bona fide?*
— Does the company provide an after-sales service?
— How big is it?
— What kinds of clients are represented?
— Give details of references from clients.
— Which distribution method is used? Wholesalers, intermediaries, retailers, direct selling etc.?
— Does the company have a network of salesmen? How big is it?
— In the case of intermediaries (i.e. middlemen) — what is the current rate of commission?
— What are the profit margins on imported goods?

— Are the commissions calculated on FOB or CIF prices?
— Why is this company interested in representing your products?
— What is the anticipated turnover in one, two, years' time etc.?
— What methods will be used? Establishment of a specialised department? Increase in the number of employees? Publicity and promotional campaigns?
Other methods?
— What trade fairs etc. does the company take part in?
— Banking and personal references.

Of course this questionnaire must be adapted to suit each company and its products. But on the whole the exporter should save a great deal of time and money by making his first selection from the answers obtained on such a questionnaire.

3.2.2 Selecting an agent

Once all the prospective agents have replied, the exporter can make his first choice by eliminating all those who did not reply to the questionnaire.

It is difficult to tell the good agent from the bad agent just from a questionnaire. As we have already pointed out the exporter should distrust his clients who wish to become agents with the sole objective of obtaining the best possible prices for anything they buy. Some agents who represent rival companies try to represent this exporting company so as to 'freeze' its products and therefore be in a better position to sell their own products or those of their principals. Some agents with a good reputation are much sought after and take on many clients. As they can only devote a small percentage of their time and effort to each product these agents often quickly become bad agents. Once this primary selection has been completed, the exporter must then try to check, as far as possible, the information received. This can be done by contacting the agents' banks, customers and other principals.

With regard to information on a company's reputation, the BOTB can help the exporter to obtain a great deal of information on a foreign company and charge only a fraction of the costs involved. It would be a pity to deprive oneself of this information through not wanting to pay such a modest fee, and risk engaging an agent after receiving incorrect information on him. British banks with branches abroad can help to check most of the banking and legal information given by the prospective agents. Once again, banks play an important part in choosing agents.

Once this information has been received and checked, the exporter is usually left with several possibilities and with the problem of actually making a final choice. The exporter should meet his potential agents before making this final decision. Visiting the agents themselves is better than being visited by them. Naturally, even if you visit them they could still visit you. In fact, the exporter can gain a personal knowledge of the prospective company by visiting its premises and some of its clients, and can, in this way, get a far better idea than through a mere questionnaire. What sales manager would hire a salesman just from reading his curriculum vitae without interviewing him? It is quite irrational not to arrange a meeting with these potential agents on the pretext of distance, expense, or time involved, because the agent will represent the exporting company throughout a particular area, usually an entire country, and a personal meeting can lead to a better understanding towards mutual benefit to both parties.

On his return to head office, the exporter can make his final decision and submit a proposal for a contract to the agent concerned. This contract, which we are now going to outline, is the document which forms the basis of the relationship and obligations between the two parties. Although within the Common Market a manufacturer does not have the right to refuse to sell goods to anyone else living within the EEC even when he has an exclusive agent in the country from where the order emanates, it is none the less true that the contract reinforces the link between the agent and the principal.

3.3 The contract

At first sight it would seem possible to prepare a contract which could be applied to all types of agents. Although this is generally the case, the different legal systems of overseas countries and the various points on which they differ must be taken into consideration. This is the reason why it has not yet been possible to draw up any truly international laws. A contract which is valid between parties of different countries can only be drawn up by making a parallel between the various laws concerned. The International Chamber of Commerce has published a 'Guide for preparing agent contracts between parties from different countries'. It is possible to envisage various kinds of contracts. A contract between a company and its agent, whether this is an individual or a legal entity, will differ depending whether he is a commission agent or an importing agent.

In the case of a commission agent certain specific clauses must be included:

— the nature of the commission;
— the rate of commission, usually calculated as a percentage of the invoiced amount (Also it must be specified whether the amount in question is FOB or CIF. On the other hand, in some contracts the commissions are graded, e.g. 10 per cent up to £100,000, 8 per cent from £100,000 to £200,000 etc. A different rate of commission is applied for each section of the contract.);
— the currency in which the commission is to be paid;
— when the commission is to be paid, at the stage of order, delivery or payment (the last is usually the case);
— is the agent *bona fide?*

As we have already seen, the commission agent has fewer ties with his supplier than the importing agent and therefore the contract will be less elaborate, often limited to a simple letter acting as a contract.

Below is a typical example of a contract with an importing

agent, and most of the clauses also apply in the case of a contract with a commission agent. In Appendix I there is an example of an identical contract in French.

EXAMPLE OF A CONTRACT WITH A FOREIGN AGENT

This agreement is made the . . . . day of . . . . 197 . . . .
between . . . . with its principal office at
. . . . hereinafter referred to as 'supplier' and
. . . . with its principal office at
. . . . hereinafter referred to as 'distributor'.

WHEREIN IT IS MUTUALLY AGREED AS FOLLOWS:

1 TERRITORY

Supplier hereby appoints distributor its distributor for the following territory: . . . .
Such appointment shall be on an exclusive basis except that supplier reserves the right to sell the goods to others for use in the territory provided that it will not exercise such right without the distributor's prior knowledge and in the event that such right be exercised compensation will be paid but the amount thereof shall be at supplier's discretion.

2 PRODUCTS

For the purposes of this agreement 'products' shall mean the products listed on appendix 1 attached to this agreement and such new products as shall be introduced from time to time by supplier provided such new products are, in the sole opinion of supplier, of the same product line as those currently being marketed by distributor under this agreement.

3 SUPPLIER HEREBY AGREES:

3.1 To sell to distributor in the described territory for the term of this agreement products defined above. On all such sales, the prices and other terms of sale shall be supplied at standard distributor price list and terms of sale for the territory as may be established from time to time by supplier . Distributor will pay to supplier the full amount of every invoice rendered to them by supplier in U.S. dollars, and upon supplier's terms of payment as detailed on the appendix hereto without deduction in respect of commission or collection of bank charges. Supplier reserves the right to specify such other terms of payment as it may deem appropriate.

3.2 To give prompt attention and consideration to distributor's orders for products, provided, however, that supplier will not be liable for any loss to distributor or any third party for delays or failures in manufacture or in delivery resulting from causes beyond the control of supplier.

3.3 To supply, at its discretion, distributor with a reasonable quantity of catalogues and sales literature for distribution. Additional literature will be supplied at cost to distributor when the demand exceeds the allowance.

4 DISTRIBUTOR HEREBY AGREES:

4.1 To devote its best efforts to promote the use and sale of products within the territory and to make diligent efforts to obtain new customers and increase sales volume each year.

4.2 To maintain an inventory of products at all times sufficient to meet an anticipated sales in the territory for the succeeding 90 days.

4.3 Not to engage directly or indirectly in the manufacture production, importation, advertisement or sale of any products in the territory which are competitive with any of the products under this agreement.

4.4 Not to advertise for customers, create branch establishments or maintain warehouses for delivery purposes outside the described territory.

4.5 To refer to supplier all orders for and enquiries about products received by distributor from sources outside the described territory.

5 DURATION

5.1 The original term of this agreement shall be from the effective date hereof to ....

and if not previously terminated, each year thereafter this agreement shall be automatically renewed for an additional period of one calendar year; provided, however, that either party may, by written notice to the other not less than six (6) months prior to the expiration of the current period, whether original or renewal, specify the end of such period as the date of termination and on such date this agreement shall terminate.

5.2 If, in the event, one party fails to comply with any of the provisions of the agreement, the other party may terminate this agreement as the result of such failure by written notice to the defaulting party specifying the nature of the failure upon which such termination is based and the agreement shall terminate thirty (30) days thereafter.

6 SALES QUOTAS AND PERFORMANCES

6.1 Distributor agrees to maintain throughout each year, a rate of sales sufficient to achieve the annual sales quota established by supplier. The sales quota for each successive year shall be determinated by supplier based upon distributor's past performance; Upon change in population; gross national product and other market conditions in the territory; and upon supplier's knowledge and experience of sales in other territories.

6.2 At supplier request, distributor shall submit a full report of market conditions within the territory including the names of firms selling competitive products and the selling prices of such and any other information.

6.3 Distributor agrees to inform supplier of its current retail prices and revisions thereof for products in the territory and provide, on a monthly basis, returns of unit sales and inventory.

6.4 Distributor agrees to allow the duly authorised representatives of supplier every opportunity of acquainting themselves with the methods and progress of sales and service carried out by distributor in the territory with a view to guiding distributor in relation to their sales and service organisation.

7 PRODUCT WARRANTY AND SERVICE POLICY

7.1 A standard printed warranty for the products is provided to the ultimate customer. Without charge, supplier agrees to repair or replace, (within the limitations provided in the printed product warranty) defective parts or components. Supplier's obligation under this warranty does not include any labour costs incident to the replacement of defective parts and distributor hereby agrees to assume any such costs.

7.2 Distributor agrees to cooperate fully with supplier in carrying out the general warranty policy on the products and, subject to the limitations of sub-paragraph (7.1) above, hereby undertakes and assumes the obligations of such warranty policy to the ultimate customer.

7.3 Distributor agrees to provide consistently high quality service for the products and shall organise and maintain throughout the territory adequate facilities and stocks of spare parts and shall employ sufficient number of competent and trained personnel as is necessary to achieve this objective.

8 ADVERTISING AND PROMOTION PROGRAMMES

8.1 Supplier may, from time to time, provide sales literature, advertising materials, promotional plans and other information and programmes to assist distributor in merchandising the products in the territory. All such literature and material shall remain the property of the supplier and, upon request, distributor agrees to return all such literature and materials to supplier free of charge.

8.2 Distributor agrees to implement and participate in any sales or promotional programmes provided by the supplier under subparagraph (8.1) above including programmes which provide for commissions bonuses, or other incentive payments to distributor's employees.

8.3 Distributor, at its own initiative, shall conduct promotional programmes to stimulate sales of products.

8.4 Distributor agrees to have a permanent display of the products in the distributor's showroom.

9 TRADE MARKS, TRADE NAMES AND PATENTS

9.1 All products marketed by distributor shall be sold only in the form packaged by supplier, and dis tributor shall not alter, modify, or change any product or its package without prior written consent of supplier.

9.2 Distributor shall not use or seek registration of any trade mark, trade name or patent owned by supplier or by any company affiliated with the supplier, except as expressly authorised in writing by the supplier. Distributor shall not challenge or contest the validity of ownership of any such trade mark, trade name or patent and shall exercise vigilance to detect and report to supplier any actual or potential infringement of such rights in the territory. Supplier shall be solely responsible for any action required to acquire, maintain, preserve or enforce its rights under such trade marks, trade names or patents, but distributor agrees to provide any assistance requested by supplier (at supplier's cost) in connection therewith.

10 TERMINATION

10.1 In the event of termination or expiration without cause, neither supplier nor distributor shall be liable to the other because of such termination or expiration for compensation, reimbursement, or damages on account of the loss of prospective profits on anticipated sales or on account of expenditures, investments, leases or commitments in connection with the business or goodwill of supplier or distributor, or for any other reason whatsoever. Distributor shall not, however, be relieved of any obligation for any unpaid balances of goods shipped hereunder prior to termination or for special goods ordered by distributor which are in the process of manufacture.

10.2 The termination or expiration of this agreement operate as a cancellation, as of the date thereof, of all orders which have not been shipped other than orders for special goods, and neither party shall thereafter be under any obligation to the other with respect to orders so cancelled.

10.3 Upon termination or expiration of this agreement; supplier has the right to re-purchase from distributor, at distributor's actual landed cost, all products then in distributor's possession which are in first class condition and saleable as new merchandise and which are not required by distributor for delivery to its customers on orders booked prior to the date of such termination or expiration.

10.4 Upon termination or expiration of this agreement, distributor agrees to deliver to supplier all records relating to services, sales and customer lists which pertain to the products; to refrain thereafter from representing itself as a distributor of supplier or using any trade names, trade marks, or in any other way representing itself as such as distributor; to forthwith change its name to any other name which does not incorporate the trade marks or trade names of the supplier; to return to supplier or immediately destroy all stationery, advertising matter and other printed material in its possession or under control containing or bearing any trade mark or trade name of supplier; and furthermore, to take all appropriate steps to remove and cancel its listing in telephone books, other directories, public records or elsewhere, which state or indicate the distributor is a distributor of the supplier.

11 NOTICES

Notices to the parties of this agreement should be sufficiently served if mailed to the following addresses. To supplier at ....

To distributor at ....

Notices sent by registered mail shall be effective as of the date of mailing; all other notices shall be effective only upon actual receipt by the addressee.

12 CONSTRUCTION

This agreement is unassignable and non-transferable by distributor. This agreement and its terms and conditions shall be governed exclusively by and construed according to the laws of the United States of America. The official text of this agreement and any schedule attached hereto or any notices given or accounts or statements required hereby shall be in English.

13 WAIVER

The failure of either party to enforce the provisions of this agreement shall not be deemed a waiver of such provisions or of the right of such party thereafter to enforce such provisions.

14 FINANCIAL STATEMENTS AND RESPONSIBILITY

Upon execution of this agreement, and at times thereafter as may be requested by supplier, distributor agrees to furnish supplier duly certified balance sheets and such other statements in sufficient details as may be reasonably required by supplier to establish to the satisfaction of supplier, the financial responsibility of distributor as provided herein. Distributor agrees that it will provide, maintain and reserve out of its total financial resources working capital funds in the amount ....
deemed by supplier from time to time to be adequate to finance properly the purchase of the products when due and to ensure the orderly and effective merchandising sale and promotion of products. Distributor shall not be entitled to enter into any contracts in the name of or on behalf of

supplier without supplier's consent in writing nor shall distributor be entitled to pledge the credit of supplier in any way.

15 NOTICE OF INTERNAL CHANGE

The parties hereto agree that, due to the close relationship involved in a distributorship agreement, supplier must necessarily rely on distributor's business experience and good reputation to adequately ensure the protection of the supplier's trade marks, reputation and goodwill therefore, distributor agrees to give supplier immediate notice in writing of any transaction affecting the ownership of its capital stock, if a corporation; or of any change in the respective interest of the partners, if a membership and, of any transaction affecting the ownership of any part of the business, if an individual.

Distributor also agrees that during the term of this agreement it will not make or suffer to be made a change of more than 50% of the ownership of distributor without first obtaining the written consent of the supplier.

16) This agreement replaces and supersedes all previous agreements, understandings or arrangements between the parties.

17) Three (3) copies of this agreement will be signed by all parties and each copy bearing the signatures of all the parties hereto shall constitute an original. However, this agreement shall be of no force and effect unless and until at least one such copy shall be signed by all parties.

Executed this . . . . day of . . . . 197 . . . .

Signed on behalf of (supplier)	signed on behalf of (distributor)

. . . .

. . . .

3.4 Visiting an agent

Visiting an agent is certainly one of the most important moments with regard to the smooth running of business relations with the agent. A great many exporters often do not bother to visit their agents as they consider it to be a waste of time and, in particular, too great an expenditure for the benefit it could bring. In a recent seminar for exporters it was clear that less than half had visited their agents abroad at least once that year. We shall now consider why, when and how a visit to an agent abroad should be carried out.

3.4.1 Why visit an agent abroad?

There are many reasons. One of the most common is that one can also visit the main potential clients with the agent. The agent can also call on the exporter to negotiate any important or delicate business transaction which requires technical or marketing assistance. He increases his chances, and as a result his principal's chances, of success by creating a real psychological impact.

One, two or even three check-up visits a year are absolutely essential. Such visits enable the exporter not only to exercise some control over the agent's work but also to provide incentive for the agent. In their book *Export Agents* Colin McMillan and Sydney Paulden very rightly remark that 'water boils better when there is a fire underneath it'. The exporter usually tends to visit his better agents. Often, it is more useful to visit those whose results are not so good so that the reasons for this can be analysed. In some cases, the agent neglects a product because he does not know enough about it. One or more training visits may prove necessary.

3.4.2 How often to visit agents

Usually it is better to arrange a visit to an agent in advance. In fact it would be most convenient for him to receive a visit from his principal during an exhibition or when the books are being audited. If the agent is veru busy he will not be able to devote sufficient time to his visitor and as a result the object of the visit is not achieved and both time and money are wasted.

The best solution is to suggest several dates and to leave it up to the agent to choose, thus putting him in an 'asking' position. Frequency of visits depends on the distance involved. One visit a year is sufficient for countries such as Brazil or Japan, but more visits should be arranged for countries in Europe. However, if the exporter feels that his agent's sales are satisfactory without ever having to visit him, this proves that the market is potentially much larger and that if the agent was given more incentives he would doubtless obtain better results.

When a new agent is engaged more visits are necessary. It is up to the exporter to appraise his agent's level of training and to decide whether another visit is necessary. The number of lightning visits which need to be made in order to see an agent cannot be exactly defined. However, one must be on one's guard against agents who are forever calling on their supplier. The exporter will in this case be more like a salesman and when he has gone the agent will file his dossier and will wait for his next visit before contacting his existing and prospective customers again. The exporter must therefore decide on the value of such a trip and should not accept unless there is a good reason. When one of the exporter's products is being exhibited by an agent he should pay a visit in order to ensure that everything is running smoothly. The exporter should spend one,two or three days at his agent's stand. It would be better to go no the last few days of the exhibition as, at the beginning of the exhibition, the agent would have very little time to spend with his principal, as he would be occupied in setting up the stand and organising the exhibits. Also the exporter would then have a better idea of the results obtained, large expected orders etc., and would be able to make a list of British and foreign customers who are interested in his product to be circulated both to his other agents and to his domestic sales department. The exporter could also suggest that the agent visits him so that he can increase his knowledge of the products by seeing where they are produced. But, however beneficial these visits may be they cannot compensate for regular visits by the exporter to his agents. The period of time spent with the agent depends entirely on the aim in mind. If the exporter visits a particular client with his agent one visit is usually enough. Check-up visits on the other hand should take two or three days. As far as training visits are concerned, the length of time depends on the type of product. The more sophisticated and technically complicated the product, the more time should be spent with the agent.

3.4.3 Organisation of the visit

Visiting an agent will only be fruitful if the visit is well organised. Before any check-up visits, certain tasks must be completed. The list below is not exhaustive and must be adapted to suit the particular business concerned.

— Read over correspondence since the last visit.

— Read over the last report made by the head of the export department, or any other member of the department, after the previous visit to this agent.

— Check to see whether the agent has recently placed any orders, whether they have been processed, when delivery is to take place etc.

— Check whether invoices made out to this agent have been settled. If not, make out a list of the unpaid invoices and obtain a copy of each one — this will spare lengthy discussions on the invoices, how much they are for etc.

— Make out a statement of the sales achieved by the agent and compare these to the forecasts made at the beginning of the year. Where renewed orders constitute the bulk of the turnover it is a good idea to make out a list of the customers who have placed their orders this year and those who have not yet done so.

— Prepare any technical or commercial sales literature which may be of use to the agent.

— Inform the agent of your visit by letter. It is also possible to ask him to contact his main existing or prospective clients so that you can both visit them.

3.4.4 The visit itself

The two or three days spent with the agent are very important not only in the sense that they represent an important investment but also because, as we noted above, the nature of your relations with the agent depends on them. We have tried to put the different points that the exporter must remember and which determine the nature of his visit, in the form of a check-list. The check-list given below is only an example and as such must be adapted to suit the circumstances. However, it is always in the exporter's interest to make out a check-list so that nothing can be forgotten.

CHECK-LIST

— Date of last visit;
— Visit made by: to:
— Current turnover:
  — Product A:
  — Product B:
  — Product C:
— Of those sales forecast, how many have been achieved to date?
— Which customers have renewed their orders this year?
— What percentage do your products represent in the agent's total turnover?
— What new products are being represented by the agent?
— Is he representing any new clients?
— Are there any new salesmen for your products?
— What new advertising and promotional campaigns has your agent begun since your last visit (mailing, exhibitions, etc.)?
— Has the sales literature on your products been translated? Does your agent have sufficient sales literature?
— Is the training of salesmen, and particularly new salesmen, adequate?
— Which goods does your agent have in stock? Make out an inventory. The exporter must as far as possible ascertain the

level of these stocks. In fact the agent will usually prefer to cut these socks to a minimum and order again when further stock is needed.

— Meet the technicians in the after-sales service department. Do they have an adequate technical knowledge of your products? Trade fairs and exhibitions are generally the best time to find this out. Where they need further training suggest a period of technical instruction at the company or send out a technician to give them further training on the spot.

— How many technical visits, i.e. those made by the after-sales service, have been made to the customers (repairs, maintenance)?

— What does the agent think of your product? What are his criticisms? It is important to take note of his remarks and criticisms and to pass them on to the relevant departments i.e. technical department, marketing department etc . . .

— What new business does the agent have? Once the exporter has received orders he certainly has, or should have, a thorough knowledge of the business. However, the very fact of discussing this business shows the principal's interest and the fact that he is closely following every transaction.

— Draw up a list of potential customers. Classify them by quantity as well as value. It is a good idea to estimate when these potential customers might actually order. One advantage gained by doing this is that sales forecasts can be adjusted throughout the year. Another is to be able to give new impetus to his agent when necessary and to ascertain whether he is doing everything he should to obtain orders. It would be even better actually to work with the agent and to ask for regular information on the state of future business rather than to have a passive role and not be well informed about the business in hand until after the order has been placed.

— During his stay, the exporter could also visit his main existing and prospective customers with his agent. An importing agent will usually be less willing to reveal the name of his customers, so it would therefore be very useful for the exporter to take a note of the information on his clients already in the files. These files increase in importance if there is a change of agent as the exporter will therefore not be caught completely unawares. Also, many customers renew orders on a regular basis or stock up with spare parts etc. By using these files the exporter can easily see which customers are renewing orders and which are not, and can examine the reasons for this.

INFORMATION TO BE ENTERED ON A CUSTOMER'S FILE (see examples in Chapter 4)

Customer's name, address and telephone number:
Nature of business:
Contact:
Potential turnover:
What competition is there for this business?
Rival products — price?
Is the customer already being provided with this line of goods?
By whom?
Number of visits made:
Additional information:
Visits to customers are usually recorded in a general report which is filed and then forgotten. The advantage of using a card-index system is that not only can one keep a card on each market but also one can avoid having to keep lengthy reports which are of only short-term interest.

Obtaining maximum information on the market and the competitor is certainly one of the most difficult points to broach with an agent. In fact, although it is quite understandable that the exporter will not always be fully informed on all future business, it is absolutely necessary for him to be acquainted with the market and competitors there. The exporter must therefore try to obtain as much information as possible on this market without actually questioning his agent directly, thus showing his ignorance which would not only discredit him in the eyes of his agent but which would enable the agent deliberately to use this lack of knowledge to his advantage. This market knowledge will be of great use in sales forecasting, studying the competitors etc. In many cases, the agent will try to minimise the importance of the market to

make it clear that he has 60 or 70 per cent of the market and that he is easily the best agent there. Presented in this way, the exporter would have no reason to change his agent and in particular, he would be in no position to judge his agent's true efficiency.
Action to take for customers visited : quotations to be determined, samples to be sent, and information to be passed on.
For potential customers : what advertising and promotional campaigns are to be carried out in the near future? What help should the exporter give the agent? Readjusting the agent's stocks etc.

3.5 Motivating the agents

Motivating agents is undoubtedly something to which the exporter should attach great importance. In fact an agent who is motivated will sell more and better than an agent who is not motivated. At a trade fair or exhibition, the agent will more willingly concede a choice place on his stand to the products of a company which provides him with the most incentives. The exporter who is marketing his products through an agent who usually has many principals is, in a way, competing with his agent's other principals even though their products do not rival his own.

There are different ways and means of motivating an agent. We are now going to try to show some of these methods.

3.5.1 Treat the agent's demands with consideration

Treating an agent with consideration means above all replying to every communication, and particularly to his correspondence as quickly as possible. Every exporter has repeated opportunities to realise that a request for information that he does not consider to be urgent, sometimes has a bearing on an important sale. The exporter can only understand the importance of his agent's requests when he pays him a visit. It is a rare thing for either exporters or agents to waste their time with unnecessary correspondence. By dealing with his agent's correspondence and enquiries quickly and efficiently, the exporter not only helps the agent but also makes him more well-disposed towards his principal.

3.5.2 Competitive prices

The first question the agent asks his future principal is the level of his prices compared to those of his competitors. The exporter's chief *raison d'être* is to sell more. The exporter does not export for the pleasure of exporting but is a businessman who is always concerned with profitability. Although this fact is recognised by all exporters they do not all admit that the agent, who is also a businessman, also wants to make a profit on sales and to make his business profitable.

Every agent, whether he is a commission or importing agent, must be in a position to be able to clear a large profit margin on the products he is marketing. This profit margin is undoubtedly the main way of motivating an agent. It is quite natural for the agent to devote most of his time and effort to those items which are most profitable to him and leave those products which are bought by his customers from time to time rather than having to be sold to them. It is often a good idea for the exporting company to devote his efforts to a few products so that he can become a 'leader' in these particular products, even if it means dropping or restricting his other products, rather than become uncompetitive throughout his whole range.

3.5.3 Catalogues and brochures

The manufacturer's catalogue is the material link between the exporter, his agents and customers. This why the exporter should never stint the quality of his catalogues and publicity brochures. Although a large company can produce brochures for each of the countries to which it is exporting, the small and medium-sized company, in the interests of economy, will only be able to produce one brochure for all the countries to which it is exporting. The exporter can leave it to his agent to produce an identical brochure in the language of his country. Very often, the agent hesitates to invest in such a brochure or produces one of mediocre quality. The answer is for the exporter to be responsible either for a percentage of the costs of preparing foreign literature, up to a state maximum, or for a sum equal to a particular percentage of the business transacted or anticipated by the agent. The sales literature must first be approved by the exporter. Another solution is to print all the literature without any text, in order to benefit from any discounts available on having a large number printed at one time. Only the photographs, diagrams and sketches are printed and sent free to the agents, who are then only responsible for reproduction costs. The advantages of such a system are numerous. Firstly the exporter can standardise his sales literature throughout the world. The format, quality and colours used will be the same whatever the country or agent. Unlike the previous solution, this one is financially advantageous for both the agent and the exporter. However, in some countries such as Spain, sales literature is subject to high import duties. Any advantage is therefore nullified.

3.5.4 Newsletters

A great many multinational groups or large companies produce newsletters or circulars for their agents and branches on a regular basis, i.e. every month. These newsletters are usually produced in the form of a glossy magazine. If a small or medium-sized company cannot assume the cost of this sort of magazine it would probably be able to produce a monthly circular letter. This letter could be printed or even roneoed or photocopied if the circulation does not warrant a large quantity.

Each newsletter must be dated and numbered. An efficient method is to print coloured folders preferably with a typed heading such as 'PATON INFORMATION', or 'NEWS'. The actual sheets will supply the information. If they are dispatched regularly they should be clearly distinguishable as that particular company's newsletters. The exporter should also send the agents an index file so that the newsletters can be bound and filed easily. These files should already be perforated to save the agent any further trouble. This will also increase the chances of their being kept.

The aim of a newsletter is to maintain a close and continuous link between the exporting company and its agents. From a psychological point of view this kind of newsletter shows the agent that the exporting company is serious in its attitude and is interested in the agent's work. As these newsletters are sent abroad they must be written in a language understood by everybody concerned. The company can inform his agent of any changes in policy and provide him with general information in these newsletters, which should be rational and should bring the following points to the agent's attention:

— new products
— results obtained abroad or even in Great Britain which would interest all his agents
— technical information on a product or on particular aspects of a product, e.g. in the case of a company specialising in the manufacture of credit cards: 'The technical aspect of the signature block', 'offset printing' etc.
— applications of the product; using the same example as above, 'the plastic card, a means of identifying patients in hospitals' etc.
— report of the last agents' seminar, the agenda and dates of the next one.

3.5.5 Seminars and training courses

Although seminars and training courses are under the same heading they must be dealt with separately. A training course is used to present the products to a new agent, both from the marketing and the technical points of view. These courses are usually organised to train one agent at a time and they take place at the exporting company's head office or at the factory. The exporter should ensure that, by the end of the course, the agent is conversant with the product and its applictions, before allowing him to market these products. In fact, as we have already pointed out, an agent with a good reputation but who is not really conversant with his new principal's products, will no doubt be a very bad agent because of this.

Seminars are instruction and training courses but they differ in the way in which they are organised. Seminars bring together a great many agents, if not all of them, and are usually held once or twice a year off the company's premises (i.e. in a country club, hotel etc.). They are more public relations exercises than training courses in the true sense of the word. General points which interest all those present are discussed. New products are presented, as are proposed publicity and promotional campaigns. By planning such a seminar towards the end of the year (October or November) the exporter and the agents can prepare sales forecasts for the next year. Serious forecasts are difficult to obtain otherwise.

The agent's wives could also be invited to both the seminar and the various entertainments organised. The exporter should take charge of all the expenses resulting from the seminar, food and acommodation for the agents, entertainment etc. The main problem in organising a seminar of this kind is obtaining sufficient numbers of participants, as some may come from countries which are a long distance away. One could combine this seminar with a specialised exhibition or trade fair which the agents normally visit anyway. Another problem is which language to use. This can usually be resolved by using English which is usually understood by everybody. The seminar's programme can either be sent to the agents or passed around at the beginning of the seminar. During these seminars the best agents can be awarded 'sales oscars', or sales competitions could be arranged. This method of encouraging agents, often used by some large companies continues to stand the test of time. They include the 'No. 1

Club', 'Quota Club', etc. Prizes such as cruises and holidays are often awarded as well as the oscars.

3.5.6 Co-operation in advertising

If the agent is unwilling to invest in sales literature, he will be even more unwilling to assume any advertising costs. At the beginning of the financial year, the exporter could suggest a plan of advertising co-operation to encourage his agent. The exporter could suggest that he puts a particular number of advertisements, depending on the countries, agents and products, in magazines or newspapers of the agent's choice. The exporter prepares 2 or 3 advertisements specifying whether they are to be printed in black or white or colour, the format and the magazines and newspapers which are to be covered by the campaign. This plan should also show the maximum expenditure that the exporter will be responsible for as far as each agent is concerned. In this kind of campaign the exporter undertakes to repay a certain percentage of the expenditure to the agent. The manufacturer's proposed advertisement should give the agent's name and address.

In the following example of cooperation in advertising the company OLGA, an American women's underwear manufacturer, suggests two kinds of advertisements. They are updated every year and can be inserted into those newsletters which we have already mentioned. Our example is of course valid for a great many widely used industrial products.

EXAMPLE OF OLGA'S PROPOSED ADVERTISEMENTS

In order to sell women's underwear . . . .
. . . . . . we recommend two different kinds of advertisement:
First, a 24-inch advertisement with three different articles on our products with a common text describing our whole range.

Second, a 10-inch advertisement with only the text as in the first advertisement.

CONTRACT FOR PLAN OF ADVERTISING COOPERATION WITH 'OLGA'

Contract coming into effect on . . . .

1 *Advertising scheduled with representative:* All advertisements must be scheduled with the Olga representative and an "Advertising Authorisation" covering each ad or series of ads prepared by him. No payment will be made by Olga unless such an "Advertising Authorisation" is on file at Olga headquarters at the time a claim is filed by the customer.

2 *Financial limits:* Payment by Olga for advertising as set forth in this policy may not exceed 5 per cent of the customer's net annual purchases of regular, full-price merchandise. When, during the course of, but before the end of the calendar year, the customer's accrued advertising credits are not sufficient to offset accrued advertising claims. Olga will pay such claims up to the 5 per cent limit of the customer's previous claendar year's purchases or (in the absence of historical data) to the 5 per cent limit of a mutually agreed upon volume goal for the current year. Any claims not paid during a calendar year because of insufficient credits will be reviewed at year's end and payment made to the very limit of the total credits for the year.

3 *Rate of participation:* Subject to the limitations set forth in this statement of policy. Olga will participate in the customer's acyual cost of newspaper space at the rate of 50 per cent. Actual cost shall include any discount or refunds which the customer may be entitled to receive from the newspaper. The basis for Olga's participation shall in no event exceed the newspaper's **maximum retail rate.**

4 *Newspapers only:* Black and white ROP newspaper space **only** in daily and Sunday newspapers with circulation audited by the Audit Bureau of Circulation, is covered under this policy. Olga pays no part of either art or mechanical production costs, nor the premium charged

for either preferred position or color. No provision is made under this policy for participation in either TV or radio.

5 *Catalogues :* Olga participates in customer-produced catalogues, special newspaper inserts and direct mail brochures at the rate of £3.00 per page per thousand circulation. Fractional pages are on a pro rata basis.

6 *Filing of claims :* The customer's claim for Olga's participation in advertising costs must be filed within 60 days after the advertisement has run. Separate claims for each advertisement or series of advertisements must be filed and accompanied by three (3) tearsheets of each advertisement. Claims set forth both the amount of space used and the net rate paid by the customer. Advertising claims are processed on the basis of date of appearance in the newspaper.

7 *Credits not carried forward :* Advertising credits accrue on a calendar basis and must be used during the calendar year in which they are earned. They may not be carried over from one calendar year to another. Claims covering advertisements run during the last two months of a calendar year and received by Olga within the customary 60 days after the advertisement has run will be charged against credits accrued in the year just ended. Such claims received more than 60 days after the advertisement has run, will, like all claims filed after the 60 day deadline, be returned to the customer unpaid.

8 *Reimbursement by check :* Claims filed in accordance with this policy will be paid by check . . . usually within 30 days, and only rarely more than 60 days following their receipt.

9 *Ad specifications :* To qualify for Olga's participation in the cost of advertising, provisions must be made for the following:

a The Olga name must appear in headlines.

b Olga trademarks (such as Suddenly Slim) identified as trademarks on Olga's garment labels, must be referred to in the headlines or copy with the customary (r) or TM.

c If Olga is to pay for any portion of the ad in which other merchandise appears, Olga's share shall be based upon the actual cost pro rata to the space percentage devoted to Olga merchandise.

d If Olga is to pay for any portion of an ad in which comp-petitive merchandise appears these regulations apply:
— no other style may be presented in a space size or illustration larger than that devoted to any Olga style
— not more than one-quarter page may be devoted to Olga styles
— only Olga girdles, bras and daywear may be presented in omnibus ads. Sleepwear and loungewear are specifically excluded.

e Olga will pay for its share of loungewear ads *only* when the Olga loungewear style or styles are advertised as a part of an "Olga collection" ad with other Olga styles. Olga pays no part of ads in which loungewear styles are advertised alone or with competitive styles.

10 Other advertising available : In addition to the newspaper advertising already described, Olga makes a variety of statement enclosures available to all customers, shipping charges prepaid by Olga. While these enclosures are made available without charge, their **cost value** will be deducted from the customer's total cooperative advertising credits which accrue at the rate of 5 per cent of annual purchases. Here is the schedule of "cost values" covering such enclosures:

	Costs per 1,000			
Type of enclosure	**Under 10,000**	**10,000-25,000**	**25,000-100,000**	**Over 100,000**
one-colour printing:				
not imprinted	3.00	not available	not available	not available
imprinted	not available	3.50	3.00	2.50
four-colour printing:				
not imprinted	7.00	not available	not available	not available
imprinted	not available	6.50	5.50	4.50

Chapter 4

Managing an Export Department

4.1 Organising the Work

4.1.1 Invitation to purchase
4.1.2 Processing orders
4.1.3 Export card-indexes

4.2 Export results and how to analyse them

4.2.1 Data and its interpretation
4.2.2 Presentation of results

4.3 Sales forecasting

Chapter 4

Managing an export department

The way in which the export department is run depends primarily on its size. It is quite obvious that an export department with 30 staff will not be managed in the same way as one with two or three staff. However, some factors, such as the marketing methods selected or the nature of the goods sold, are common to all departments whatever their size.

The head of the export department must have all the information necessary for him to be able to evaluate the state of a particular market, a specific product etc. Therefore, a firm but not inflexible organisation must be achieved. Information on sales achieved, including orders and invoiced sales, estimated sales, competitors etc. must be carefully filed in a card-index or any other system which is easy to use. Having taken into account the differences between each market, their size and therefore the various possibilities open to him, the exporter must then try to follow a previously established line of direction and have a particular objective in mind.

As the export department is usually completely independent of other departments within the company, it is a firm within a firm. The exporter must therefore behave in the same way as the managing director of a company and must not be satisfied just with the fact that his own department is running smoothly but must also always keep in mind the profitability of the export department.

4.1 Organising the work

4.1.1 Invitation to purchase

The export invitation must be particularly well attended to because one is addressing foreign buyers who sometimes live several thousand kilometres away, do not speak the same language and do not always have the same commercial outlook as the exporting company. In Great Britain a visit by a salesman may assist the invitation to purchase. Taking into account the distances involved this is often impossible or at least very difficult abroad. The prime role of the invitation is to sell. The invitation is therefore of paramount importance. It can either be presented on the company's headed notepaper or even in the form of a proforma invoice. The proforma which is often demanded by many customers, is sometimes necessary where import licenses are required to import goods into some countries. This is usually the case when importing certain goods into countries like Spain or Algeria.

The exporter should prepare his quotations in English and French and any other languages necessary so as to ensure that they are fully understood by the potential buyer. The importance of the quotation depends on the nature of the product to be sold. In some cases, technical information on, or a description of, the product can be attached to the invitation to purchase or the quotation itself. Here we shall just look at the information need when proposing a particular price or quotation.

First of all it must make some reference to the customer's demand. The exporter must try not to use terms peculiar to his company only, or even to his country, i.e. reference numbers, standards etc., unless these reference numbers are accompanied by detailed descriptions. The price indicated should always show the FOB (port of embarkation) price. In the case of CIF (port of arrival) prices, the transport and insurance costs should appear separately.

The exporter should keep a copy of all the quotations

issued. These should be filed by month, country or agent so that they can be found and used immediately when an order is placed. In the case of a telephone call it is impossible to look up the quotation in the company's export files; not so in the case of a card-index system of this kind. These quotations can be grouped together so that they are easy to find and the customers or agents who were issued these quotations can be found immediately. The exporter will then be able to see how many quotations develop into orders and how many do not. Those which do not are then filed in a 'competitors' file, if the name of the competitor is known. Quotations are therefore very important when establishing short-term sales forecasts. To forecast on a short-term basis a number of ratios must first be determined. One of the most important ratios is that between the quotations which have been substantiated by orders over a particular period of time, e.g. six months, and the total number of quotations made over a period of similar length.

QUOTATIONS SUBSTANTIATED BY ORDERS
TOTAL QUOTATIONS ISSUED
(over a period of X months)

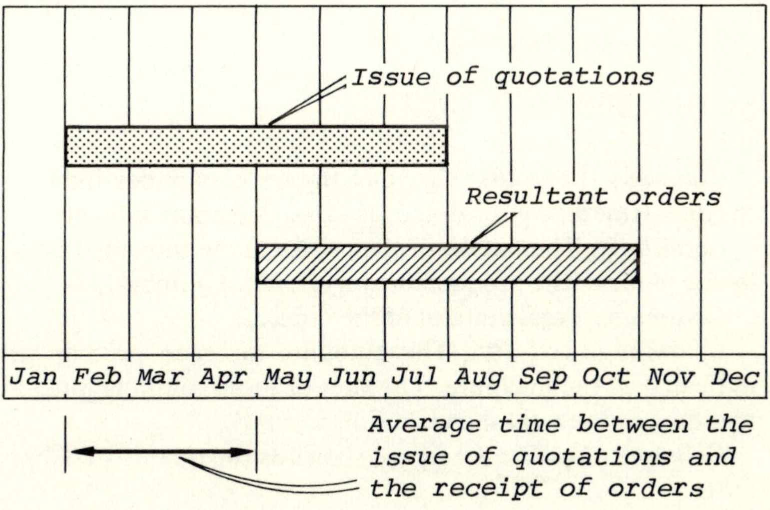

The exporter must estimate the average period between dispatching the quotation and receiving the resultant order. Let us assume that this period is 3 months and that the exporter calculates the orders which may be placed as a result of a quotation issued, between May and October. The denominator of the ratio or the total quantity of quotations issued, should therefore be calculated over the period from the beginning of February and the end of July.

Actually checking this ratio over a continuous period of time, i.e. several years, makes short-term sales forecasting much easier as long as the ratio is fairly stable.

TABLE 1.

EXAMPLE OF AN EXPORT ORDER BOOK

					TURNOVER					QUANTITIES				
ORDER NO/	NATURE OF ORDER	AGENT	COUNTRY	TOTAL	PRODUCT					PRODUCT				
					1	2	3	—	n	1	2	3	—	n
2783														
1	2	3	4	5	6	7	8	9	10	11	12	13	14	15

NOTES

Column 1 : The first figure of the order number indicates the department, e.g. 1 - domestic sales, 2- Export sales etc.

Column 2 : The nature of the order can be indicated either by the name of the product or by a reference number.

Column 5 : Total amount of the order.

Columns 6 and 10 : The amounts for each product are indicated in each column. The sum of these columns must be the same as the total shown in Col. 5.

Columns 11 to 15 : the figure shown is the quantity sold per order.

The exporter calculates his quotations over a particular period of time (3 months in our example), a total to which he then applies the percentage determined by the ratio. This calculation can be by value or by quantity. Any quotations which deviate too far from the average must be eliminated from these calculations. A quotation which is 100 times greater than the others would completely falsify the result. The quotations can be arranged in groups according to the sum involved, in order to improve the reliability of any short-term sales forecasting.

4.1.2 Processing orders

Just as the invitation to purchase differs from one company to another, and from one product to another, the methods of processing orders also differ from one company to another. However, there are certain stages which are common to all the various different methods and which help the exporter to process orders efficiently.

The order must be recorded as soon as it is received. This can be done in three different stages which are all necessary but which do not have the effect of submerging the export department in too much red tape.

Firstly, the order should be recorded in an order book in such a way that the head of the export department can find it quickly and easily. Taking the example of the order book in Table 1 on page 94, the head of the export department can always see how many orders are recorded overall, by countries, products etc., both by quantity and by value. To do this he need only have to add up the amounts entered in the particular column he is interested in. Secondly, the order must be referred to the technical departments concerned, whether it is a case of material to be manufactured or of goods which must be supplied from available stocks. A work sheet or a directive to open the order is then issued. This includes the necessary information for the manufacture of the goods, delivery, dispatch and invoicing.

TABLE 2. EXAMPLE OF 'OPENING AN ORDER'

EXPORT | OPENING OF ORDER | REF/NO. . . . DATE . . . .

Name and address of customer . . . . Old customer ☐
. . . . ☐
Customer's account no. . . . . Customer's ref. no . . . .
(to be quoted on invoice)
Address for delivery . . . . Date of delivery . . . .
. . . .
. . . .
Method of delivery [road] [rail] [sea] [air] [post] [other]
Terms of delivery
Forwarding agent to be used

Method of payment [cheque] [draft] [cash] [30 days] [60 days] [90 days]

☐ against documents . . . .
☐ against a documentary credit . . . .
☐ on delivery . . . .
☐ in cash at time of order . . . .
☐ other method . . . .

Name and address of bank . . . .

Invoice currency . . . .
Commission to be paid after goods are paid for . . . .
No. of account and address of bank . . . .

Additional information to be attached to invoice . . . .
. . . .
. . . .
Other information . . . .
. . . .

NATURE OF THE ORDER

Product code	Description of merchandise	Quantity	Unit price	Total

It should also include all the necessary addresses, delivery dates, amounts to invoice, methods of payment and other similar details (see table 2 on page 96).

Thirdly, the order must be recorded on a wall-chart. The detachable card-index will vary depending on how the work is progressing in the case of goods which have to be manufactured. The aim of such a schedule is to keep the dates when the orders should be dispatched in full view. If the export department only has a few orders in hand, this wall-chart could be replaced by a simple bills-receivable book where duplicates of orders can be filed.

4.1.3 Export card-indexes

The card-index is a fundamental tool to which the exporter often has recourse. The card-index is only useful for the company's different departments if it can be used quickly. Therefore, it must be updated regularly. As it will often be used the card-index must be boxed and be as rigid as its desired life-time necessitates.

We are not going to discuss the physical nature of the index here, but will try to study at least two examples of the way in which a 'customer's file' is established. This 'customer's file' is even more important if the goods are marketed through a network of importing agents. In fact, if the exporter decides to change his agent he will at least have information on existing and potential customers, if not on the market itself. Although he might be able to find the names and addresses of some customers in either the files or the agent's correspondence, the actual fact of having to search them means that resumption of business in that country will be considerably delayed.

The 'customer's file' will differ depending on the nature of the goods to be sold and the marketing methods to be used. In our first example (for West Germany) the exporting company sells office equipment through a network of importing agents. When the exporter visits his agent and particularly if he accompanies him on visits to the customers, he must try to find out who has ordered what, and when? He should also try to find out when the next order is anticipated and what it is for. This will be even easier if the equipment or merchandise is likely to be replaced (e.g. printed matter, calendars, toys, Christmas goods, clothes etc.). The exporter should also be able to check his agent's sales forecasts more easily by using this customer's file.

In our second example (Brazil) the exporting company sells machine-tools with a high VAT rating. The 'customer's file' can then be substituted for a file for potential customers who have been visited. This card will be of more use in the sales department than in the administrative department, and any information which may be of interest to the salesman must be entered on it as well as the customer's tastes and particular points of interest, dates of visits, rival products etc.

Other files, such as the 'competitor's file' would also be of use to the exporter. They are often used in trade departments, and they are filed by product and/or rival product. In exporting, problems arise from the third variable: the foreign country where the transactions are to take place. The same product is not always sold at the same price in Germany as Japan. Transport costs, customs duties, agents' commissions, all have to be taken into account. The price of the competitors' products should be calculated on arrival in the foreign country in question. These prices should be calculated not only in terms of these three variables, but also by taking into account that, in the case of transportation by air, co-rates or preferential tariffs which may be applied for some destinations, do not necessarily apply for others; and that the customs duties which apply to merchandise imported into country *x* are not always the same for an identical product imported into country *y*. This is particularly true for countries belonging to economic groups such as the EEC, the Commonwealth, the Andean Pact, the UDEAC, etc. Moreover, the calculation can only be made if the exporter knows the ex-works or FOB (port of embarkation) price of the rival products.

Card-indexes can be arranged by rival product and by country. The amounts shown may be in a money of account such as the franc or the US $ or even, and this is preferable, in

Example of a customers file

CUSTOMER: *NECKERMANN Gmbh* *Kaiserstrasse 12* *STUTTGART* *Federal Republic of Germany*				**'COUNTRY:** *Federal Republic of Germany* **SPECIAL INFORMATION:**				
Date of Order	Order No.	Agent	Description	Quantity	Unit Price	Total Price	Agent's Commission	Renewal of order Expected
4.10.72	*25432*	*MULLER*	*METAL SHELVES*	100	*286*	*2360*	—	*2/73*
4.10.72	*25433*	*MULLER*	*WOODEN SHELVES*	*25*	*530*	*13350*	—	*2/73*
14.12.72	*25599*	*MULLER*	*OFFICE EQUIP-MENT*			*525*	—	?
12.2.73	*78672*	*BRAWWER*	*PLASTIC LAMPS*	*250*	*112*	*28000*	*2800*	*12/73*

Example of a 'Customers File'/Brazil

NAME....................................	TOWN....................................	COUNTRY........................BRAZIL ....
ADDRESS..............................	TELEX	TELEPHONE..................
MANAGER............................	WORKFORCE	TURNOVER ....

PRODUCTION

TYPE
QUANTITY

PEOPLE CONTACTED	THEIR POSITION	DATES	PHYSICAL AND PERSONAL ASPECT

contacts	J	F	M	A	M	J	J	A	S	O	N	D	contacts	J	F	M	A	M	J	J	A	S	O	N	D
1972													1975												
1973													1976												
1974													1977												

MACHINES

TRADE MARK	TYPE	NUMBER	AGE	TRADE MARK	TYPE	NUMBER	AGE

the local currency. The countries in question will be those which are of interest to the exporter. The prices of the merchandise will be CIF (customs paid) port of arrival (e.g. the capital or the country's most important town) and this of course depends on the different methods of transport available. No agent's commissions should be included in this sum. On the second type of file (by country) — see the example below — the amounts shown are the prices which the competitors charge in that country. This is why it is useful to put down all the amounts in the local currency. Therefore, when a transaction is being negotiated, he will be able to decide, by looking at the competitor's prices, and the commission usually taken by the agents, the price which will be charged for the merchandise and the bottom price which the competitor could not undercut without damaging his profit margins too much. All this information is essential for getting to know the foreign market and for keeping a close check on it.

Competitor's File

Description of rival products	Manufacturer	Origin	FOB price (origin)	France franc	Germany D/M	Italy L	Austria S A
Product: PATON	PATON	G.B.	1725	15,000	8750	etc . . .	
PRODUCT A							
PRODUCT B							
PRODUCT C							
PRODUCT -							
PRODUCT n							

NOTES: Line 1 — Product: PATON in relation to the products of those exporting companies which are competitors in the field.

FOB price (origin) — the price shown is in the local currency; the £ sterling in the case of PATON.

Products A, B, C, etc . . . . are shown by their trade name and are competing with the PATON product.

The currencies used in the other columns are the local currencies of each country: francs for France, Deutsch Mark for Germany etc . . . .

4.2 Export results and how to analyse them

4.2.1 Data and their interpretation

Like any other department within a company, the export department should be able to examine the state of its operations at any given moment and be able to interpret it if it has all the necessary data. Whatever data the head of the export department requests are passed on to him regularly by the company's accounting and statistical departments. In this way the exporter should be in a position to be able to keep a permanent check on how far present results are moving toward's the company's objectives. This constant checking helps to reduce any deviations and to take any corrective measures which may be necessary, in plenty of time. Such analysis of data helps the exporter to base his marketing policy on a specific situation which is very likely to occur.

Orders and turnover : The exporter must separate recorded orders from invoices, particularly when the goods cannot be supplied from existing stocks and when delivery is therefore likely to take several months.

Business in hand, in the form of orders, (turnover to invoice) can easily be determined by applying the following formula:

orders at the end of. . . . . (previous month) from May
\+ orders for the month of. . . . . from June
— invoice for the month of. . . . . from June
orders in hand at the end of . . . . from June

Figure 7 (see Section 4.2.2 — presentation of results) shows the monthly analysis of orders. We have decided to analyse the orders rather than the invoices (turnover) because, although the exporter can directly affect the position of orders, he cannot affect the invoices. Although invoices result from orders, they depend only on the delivery dates prescribed by the production department.

In our example, (Figure 7) one can see some large variations (both positive and negative) from the average order. These variations are usually due to seasonal phenomena (see page 5 — improved sales distribution) and should be reduced as far as possible. In order to prevent the level of orders from becoming too low action should be taken before such a drop occurs. This action could take the form of a publicity campaign, promotion sales or mailing.

Unlike orders, the turnover (invoiced amount) is worked out for the exporter by his accounting department. However, it can only be used in statistical analysis when it is compared to the previous year's turnover, and to the projected turnover (see 'presentation of results'). The turnover can be broken down by product, country, agent etc. depending on what information is required. As an example, Graph 2 (a histogram of sales by countries) shows the extent of the exporter's dependence on the German market. However, the more the ratio $\frac{\text{agent's turnover}}{\text{country turnover}}$ moves towards position 1, the more the exporter is tied to the agent as far as results are concerned.

Analysing ratios such as $\frac{\text{turnover for new clients}}{\text{total export turnover}}$ and $\frac{\text{turnover for old clients}}{\text{total export turnover}}$ enables the exporter to judge the quality of the canvassing and of the system of following-up customers. However, if one separates the idea of old and new clients certain problems could arise especially where the goods are being marketed through a network of importing agents. The 'customer factor' can then be replaced by the 'agent factor'. In the case of a small or medium-sized company with a limited range of products, the profitability of each product can be followed by looking at the average price charged $\left(\frac{\text{turnover}}{\text{quantity}}\right)$

Costs : Only the export department's own costs should be taken into account. They include:

— wages (including social insurance charges);
— rent;
— telephone and telex;

— travelling expenses;
— advertising and promotion expenses;
— seminars and training courses etc.;
— financial costs (unpaid debts, premiums etc.).

The turnover, which is a basic factor, is only of real interest when linked to costs. The cost/turnover ratio must be examined each year but above all, over a period of several years (see Figure 4)

FIGURE 4

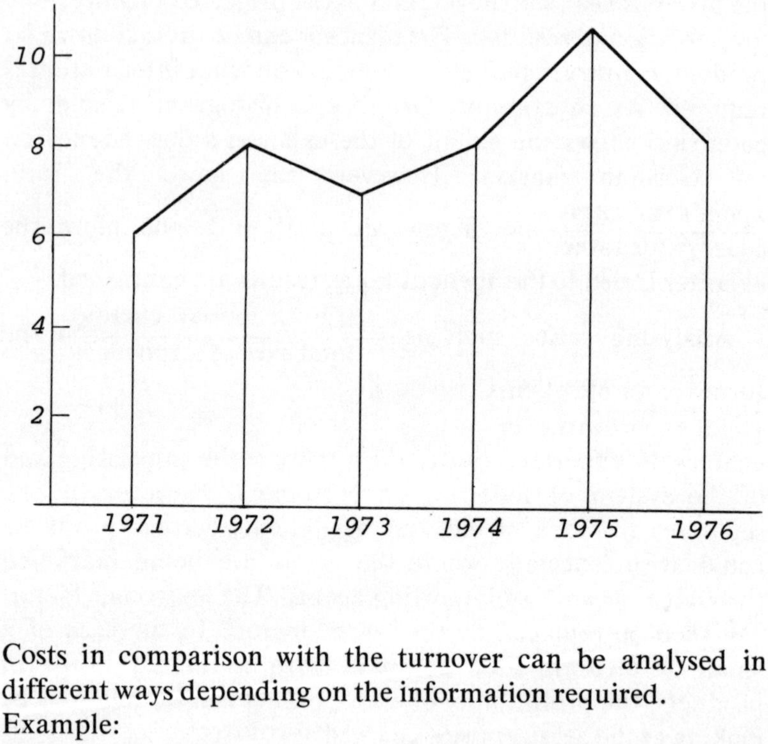

Costs in comparison with the turnover can be analysed in different ways depending on the information required.

Example:

$$\text{efficiency of the workforce} = \frac{\text{wages (social insurance paid)}}{\text{export turnover}}$$

$$\text{effectiveness of travelling} = \frac{\text{travelling expenses}}{\text{export turnover}}$$

Many ratios can be determined in this way, but they can only be used effectively when compared over a period of time.

Cost price : Two points must be taken into consideration. Firstly the expenses unrelated to the export department and then those expenses which fall to it.

— *Expenses unrelated to the export department*

These include all those expenses resulting from the production of the goods (raw materials, tools etc.), in other words the transfer price of these goods to the export department.

— *Expenses related to the export department*

This is essentially a question of commissions paid to the agents. The costs mentioned above are not included. In fact the cost/turnover ratio is only of use if the commissions are subtracted from the turnover but not added to the costs, even though this could seem to be more logical.

Example: sales throughout one year of goods at a price of 200 at a cost of 10.

In the first case, the importing agents buy from their principal (the exporter) at a discount of 50 per cent. The cost/turnover ratio is therefore 10 per cent. In the second case, the exporter sells directly at the tariff price (200) and pays his agents a 50 per cent commission. If the commission was added to the costs it would distort the interpretation of the ratio. In fact, costs 10 + commissions of 100 = 110, i.e. a cost ratio of 55 per cent.

In addition, if the commissions were not taken into account any interpretation of the ratio (cost/turnover = 5 per cent) would be distorted.

Therefore, the commissions must be deducted from the turnover before any ratios are determined.

4.2.2 Presentation of results

The data, and their static and evolutive intrepretation, enable the exporter to evaluate his particular position at a given moment when the principal objective is the profit margin.

The prime factor, the export profit margin, equals the turnover minus the export department's expenses: marketing expenses, cost price of the merchandise and the agent's commissions.

As with any other datum, the profit margin, which can be calculated both statistically and evolutively, can be broken down by agents, countries, products etc. (see Figure 5.2 — histogram of the profit margins by countries). Just as many ratios can be formed with the turnover factor, many can also be formed using the profit margin factor. This all depends on the required objective.

Example:

$$\text{profitability of expenditure on a particular country} = \frac{\text{Profit margin in that country}}{\text{Expenditure on that country}}$$

The principal ratio is still the profitability of exporting, i.e.

$$\frac{\text{Profit margin}}{\text{turnover}}$$

The results are presented in the form of tables and graphs. A simplified summary table or operations account should show the following data: turnover costs and cost price of the merchandise together with the results or profit margin.

Table 3.

1975 Export Results
Turnover

K.F.	General export results	Product A	B	C	D	E	—	n
1974 turnover	14899	6580	545	1965	3271	2176	—	1099
December 1975	2152	218	530	620	101	1850	—	254
Total 1975	19649	7282	1160	1887	2297	6994	—	1050
turnover increase as a % of 1974 values	+31.9	+10.65	+112	−4	—29.8	+221.5	—	−4.5
accumulated forecasts	18800	—	—	—	—	—	—	—
Deviation from forecasts	+4.3%	—	—	—	—	—	—	—
1974 gross profit margin	5364	—	—	—	—	—	—	—
1975 gross profit margin	7845	3416	4569	961	−660	461	—	471
increase as a % of 1974 values	46.3	46.9	39.3	50.9	−28.8	65.9	—	44.8
Projected gross profit margin	8000	—	—	—	—	—		—
Deviation from forecast profit margin	−155	—	—	—	—	—	—	—
% deviation from forecast margin	−1.9%	—	—	—	—	—	—	—

Table 4.

1975 Export Results
Quantity Sold

	Product A	B	C	D	E	—	n
1974	3020	563	2160	1930	2021	—	—
December 1975	187	102	120	76	72	—	—
Total 1975	2590	942	1830	1093	9580	—	—
% increase	– 14.2	+67.5	—15.6	+43.4	+376	—	—
Total forecast	—	—	—	—	—	—	—
Deviation	—	—	—	—	—	—	—
Deviation on forecasts as a %	—	—	—	—	—	—	—
Average price 1974	2179	968	910	1675	1082	—	—
Average price 1975	2872	1231	1031	2100	730	—	—
Deviation from average price	+633	+263	+121	+405	– 352	—	—
Deviation from average price as a % of 1974 values	+29	+27.2	+13.3	+23.9	– 32.5	—	—

Table 5. Export results by countries

General Result	1973 turnover 14899	1974 turnover 19649	forecasts 31.9%	18800	deviation 849	gross margin 7845	% gross margin 40%	expenditure 2485	3.16%	deviation from average +	profit margin for country 5360
Algeria	462	543	17,5	—	—	342	63	41	8,34	+	+ 301
Belgium	657	879	34	—	—	346	39,4	79	4,33	+	+ 267
Brazil	147	614	316	—	—	305	49,8	66	4,62	+	+ 239
France	1 413	2 346	66	—	—	961	40,1	75	12,8	—	— 886
Fed. Repub. of Germany	1 847	4 975	169	—	—	2 026	40,7	410	4,94	+	+ 1 616
Italy	1 959	2 400	22,5	—	—	716	29,8	284	2,52	—	— 432
Netherlands	1 471	1 596	8,59	—	—	695	43,5	179	3,88	+	+ 516
Portugal	178	997	458	—	—	264	26,6	85	3,10	—	— 179
South Africa	711	407	—42,3	—	—	184	45,4	375	—0,49	—	— 191
Spain	1 406	738	—47,5	—	—	349	47,3	205	1,7	—	— 144
Sweden	786	427	—45,6	—	—	250	46,8	76	2,63	—	— 124
Switzerland	896	1 064	18,7	—	—	512	48,2	96	5,33	+	+ 416
U.S.A.	1 733	1 361	—21,5	—	—	491	36	474	7,03	—	— 17
Others	—	—	—	—	—	—	—	—	—	—	—

Margin of operation = Gross profit margin/expenditure

Figure 5.1: Histogram of Sales turnover by country

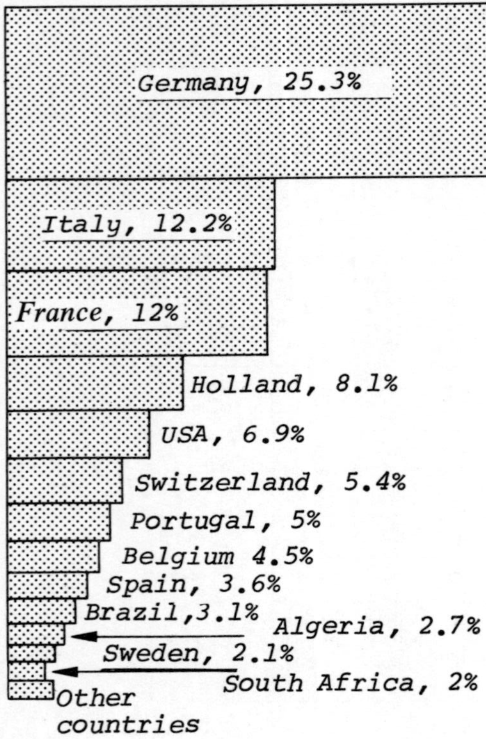

Figure 5.2: Histogram of profit margins by country

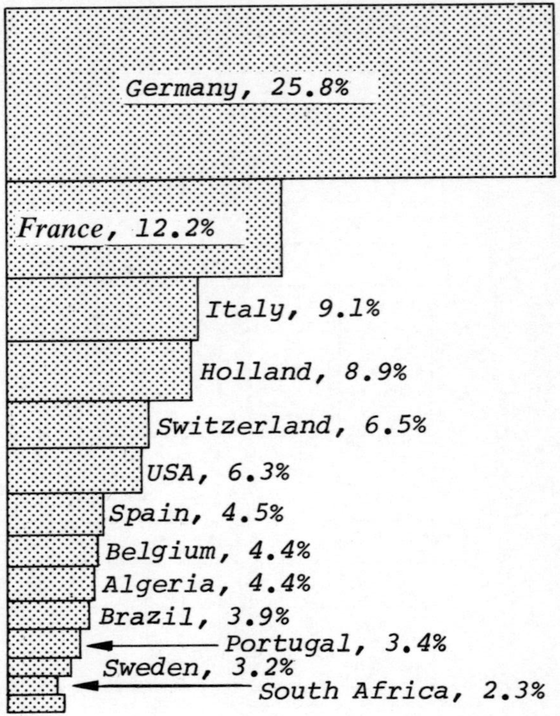

Figure 6: Showing changes in turnover

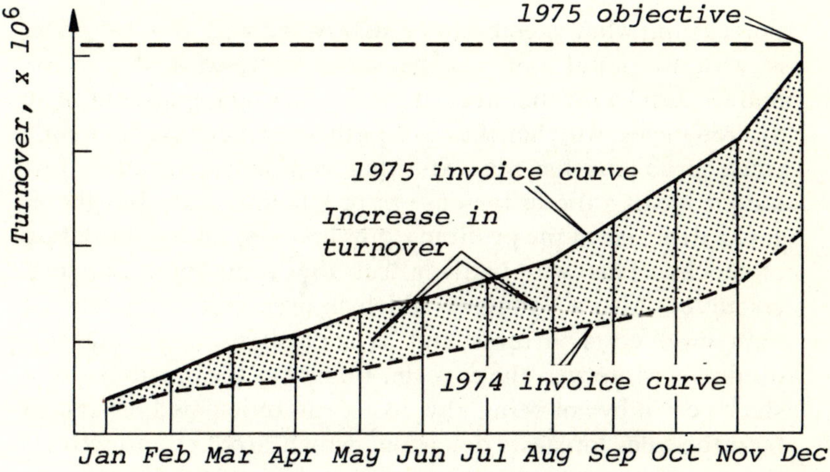

Figure 7: Monthly distribution of export orders

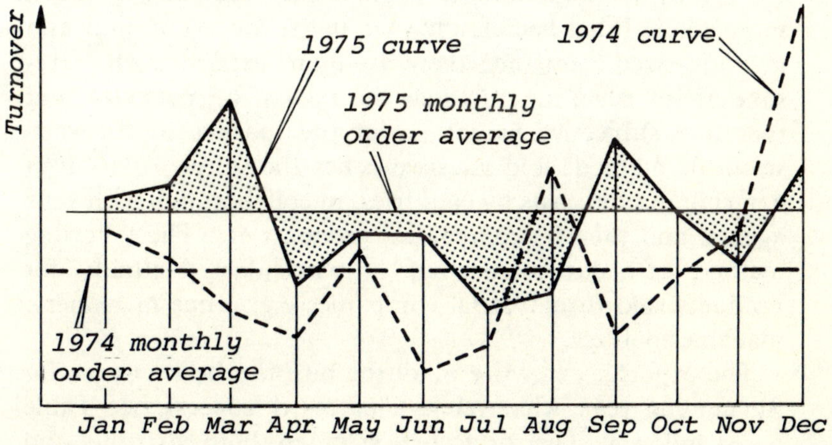

4.3 Sales forecasting

Forecasting what is going to be sold, when and at what price, is without doubt one of the most complex tasks to be undertaken by the manager of the marketing deparment. Any discrepancies, whether they are positive or negative, can only cause problems for the exporting company. Negative deviations mean a direct increase in production costs and therefore a decrease in the profit margins and also an accumulation of stocks. This will badly affect the company's financial resources. Also a company which is over-producing sees its manpower costs increase and as a result its profit margins diminish. Moreover, the exporter then risks the possibility of a slack period by not being able to accept anticipated orders. In fact, the sales forecasts determine which production methods the company puts into operation both from the points of view of the workforce and equipment.

Different scientific methods can be employed to calculate sales forecasts: the method of least squares, exponential smoothing etc. We are not going to deal with these mathematical methods here as books such as *Short-term forecasting* by Dr Zujdenweber explain such methods in much more detail. It has been found that, in the context of small and medium-sized companies there are many exporters who foresake these scientific methods in favour of personal and therefore subjective valuations of the market. In between scientific methods and guesswork lies the simple solution of determining forecasts by countries, in collaboration with your agents, and then by companies, products etc. The following method of sales forecasting is particularly suitable for products sold to industrial companies e.g. office machinery, machine-tools etc.

The exporter can write in all the business he envisages for the coming year, whatever its chances of success (see Table 6 as follows). The projected sales to both existing and potential customers are shown. However the exporter only has

Table 6. EXAMPLE OF SALES FORECAST CARD FOR A PARTICULAR COUNTRY

Australia	Total Forecasts			£
	Forecast Turnover	% of success	Forecasts	Month Forecast
Product A				
— Miller & Co..	1500	90	1350	Sept.
— Mayers & Co.	7900	70	5530	May
— Tharend Ltd.	1200	10	120	April
— Lawrence Ltd.	700	50	350	May
— Gordhens Corp.	1800	30	540	Feb
— Browns Ltd.	5000	80	4000	October
— Bryers	3500	70	2450	March
— Silverman Co.	1500	20	300	April
Total A			14640	
Product B				
— Lawrence Ltd	350	10	35	May
— Therence	1400	75	1050	Jan
—	. . . .	. . . .	. . . .	. . . .
—	. . . .	. . . .	. . . .	. . . .
Product C				
—	. . . .	. . . .	. . . .	. . . .
—	. . . .	. . . .	. . . .	. . . .

a certain percentage chance of succeeding with any order, so this particular percentage may be applied to the forecast figures. The sum of the amounts thus obtained can give a quite precise idea of future sales. This same method can be applied month by month, product by product etc. The first advantage is being able to cross-check, so that one can judge the real situation. The second is being able to follow, throughout the year, the progression of the differences between forecasts and real sales.

The same method can be applied to obtain either pessimistic or optimistic calculations. The difference between the minimum and the maximum forecasts is then obtained. The maximum can be considered as the aim to be achieved. The exporter can then reduce the difference between minimum and maximum forecasts by looking at other data such as : quotations issued, previous year's results and market trends. The total forecast for each country can be added together to give the global forecast for the export department.

By carefully following the results and comparing them with forecasts, the exporter can update his projections during the course of the year, if this proves to be necessary. There are many means at his disposal, graphs, charts, for him to do this. These aids provide a constant visual picture of the state of orders compared to the forecasts and mean that rapid action can be taken as soon as the smallest deviation occurs or is going to occur.

Example of a chart showing differences between actual and forecast sales

In Figure 7 (page 117), the forecasts are determined by country, product, agent etc. The basic unit used should not be the turnover but the percentage of forecast sales actually achieved.

Example: The exporting company, Paton, manufactures three products which it markets personally, either by mail or through a network of agents.

Table 7 *Analysis of sales forecasts by product and by country*

	Total	Product A	Product B	Product C	Product —
Export Forecasts					
Country 1					
2					
3					
4					
—					
——					
n					

Table 8 *Analysis of sales forecasts by product and by month*

	Total	Product A	Product B	Product C	Product —
Export Forecasts					
January					
February					
March					
April					
May					
June					
July					
August					
September					
October					
November					
December					

The total projected turnover is 500 and its distribution is shown in the table given below.

Table 9 *Lay-out of data for use in updating the chart showing the differences between actual and forecast sales each month.*

May 1975	Annual Forecast turnover	Forecast turnover at at the end of May	Turnover achieved at the end of May	% Forecast at the end of May	% achieved at the end of May
Total turnover	500	220	210	44	42
Product A	100	30	30	30	30
Product B	250	100	80	40	32
Product C	150	90	100	60	67
Italy	80	20	12	25	15
France	100	60	60	60	60
Scandinavia	40	10	8	25	20
Germany	70	30	32	43	76
Portugal	20	15	16	75	80
U.S.A.	60	40	20	25	33
Benelux	60	20	25	33	42
Spain	40	15	20	37	50
Other countries	30	10	17	33	5

Figure 7
Monthly control chart of actual and forecast sales

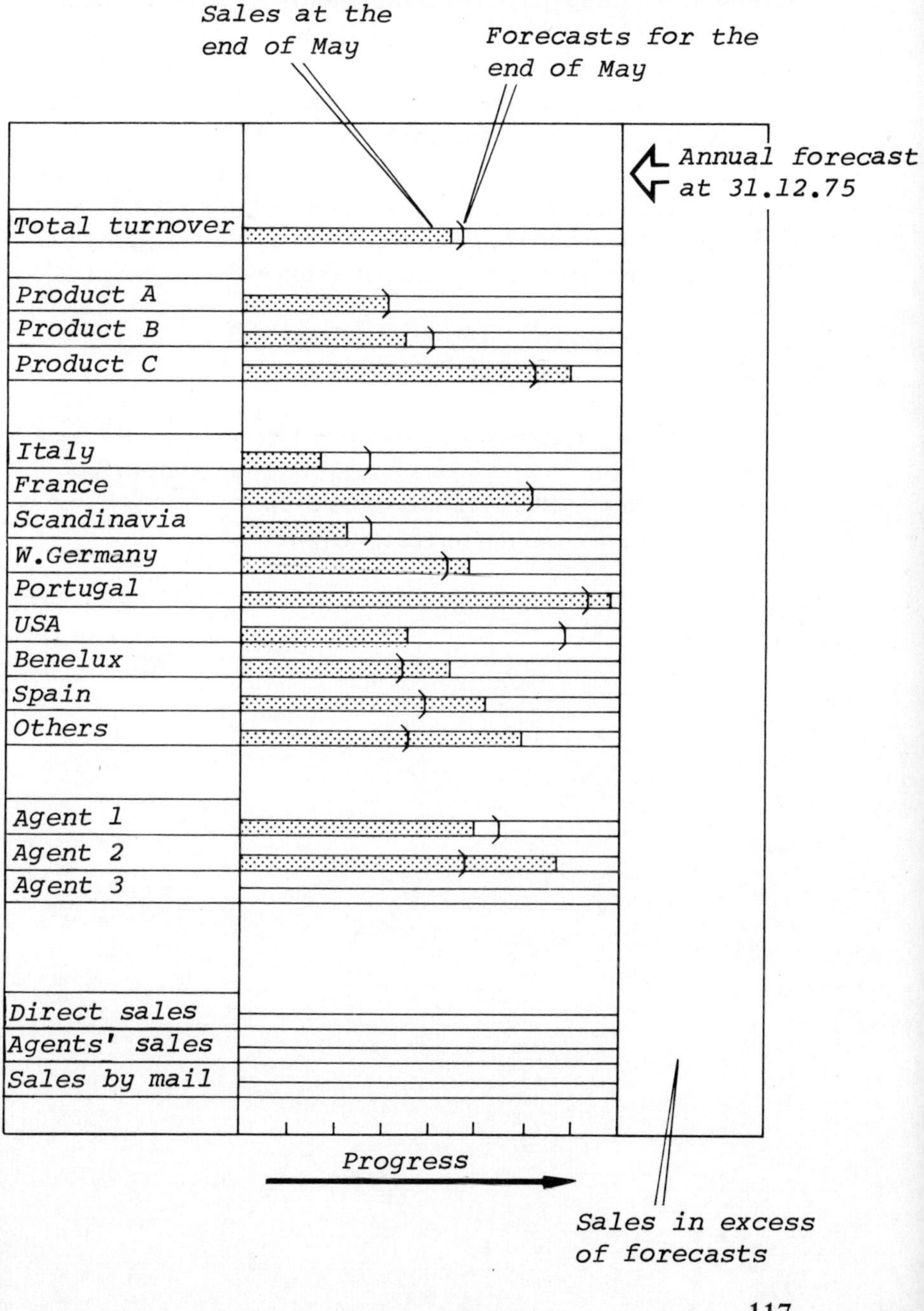

The control chart comprises coloured strips which can be moved horizontally and other lines crossing these strips which represent the forecasts at the end of month X. Actual sales are shown by moving these horizontal strips towards the vertical line representing the annual forecast for all the products, countries, agents etc. On 31 December 1975 all the vertical forecast lines on the horizontal strips will be on the final vertical line to the right of the chart as they represent the accumulated forecasts for the year. The monthly accumulated forecasts are not determined by value but as a percentage of the annual forecast (see column 4 of Table 9):

$$\frac{\text{forecast turnover at the end of X}}{\text{annual forecast turnover}}$$

The monthly accumulated sales are also determined as a percentage of the annual forecast turnover. (see column 5)

$$\frac{\text{turnover at the end of X}}{\text{annual forecast turnover}}$$

1 Example of an agents's contract in French

2 Example of a company participating in an exhibition in the USSR

3 Some books dealing with exporting

4 Useful addresses

Contrat de concession de vente

Entre

....

Le CONCEDANT
d'une part

....

Et

....

Le CONCESSIONNAIRE
d'autre part,

....

Il a été convenu ce qui suit:

Sommaire

CONDITIONS GENERALES
CONDITIONS PARTICULIERES

CONDITIONS GENERALES

ARTICLE I — OBJET DU CONTRAT:

Le CONCEDANT confére un CONCESSIONNAIRE, qui accepte, le droit de vendre les biens décrits aux "CONDITIONS PARTICULIERES" et ci-aprés dénommés le "produit contractuel". Cette concession de vente est accordée à titre exclusif.

ARTICLE II — TERRITOIRE:

Le CONCESSIONNAIRE ne pourra vendre le produit contractuel qu'à des acheteurs qui en auront l'utilisation dans le territoire défini aux "CONDITIONS PARTICULIERES".

Dans le cas où le CONCESSIONNAIRE aurait la perspective d'une vente du produit contractuel destiné à être utilisé par l'acheteur dans un pays extérieur à ce territoire, il en informera le CONCEDANT qui lui indiquera si et à quelles conditions cette vente peut être réalisée et le mettra en rapport, le cas échéant, avec le représentant ou le concessionnaire habilité pour le pays considéré.

ARTICLE III — RAPPORTS JURIDIQUES DU CONCEDANT ET DU CONCESSIONNAIRE

Le CONCESSIONNAIRE agira de maniére indépendante.

En conséquence, le CONCESSIONNAIRE passera ses commandes au CONCEDANT, en son nom et sous sa responsabilité.

Vis-à-vis de ses clients et des tiers en général, le CONCESSIONNAIRE, agissant en qualité de revendeur, recevra les commandes en son nom et pour son compte, en effectuera la livraison et en facturera le prix aux mêmes conditions.

ARTICLE IV — CONDITIONS APPLICABLES AUX VENTES DU CONCEDANT AU CONCESSIONNAIRE:

4-1: **Prévision de vente:**

Le présent contrat de concession est conclu sur la base d'une prévision d'un minimum de commandes du CONCESSIONNAIRE au CONCEDANT pour la période de référence, selon les dispositions des "CONDITIONS PARTICULIERES" (Quota de Vente).

4-2: **Rémunération de CONCEDANT:**

4-2-1: *Prix de vente:* La data d'établissement et le montant du prix de vente sont indiqués aux "CONDITIONS PARTICULIERES".

Le prix de vente inclut tous les frais et charges jusqu'au lieu de livraison au CONCESSIONNAIRE.

Il est exprimé en francs francais (monnaie de compte et monnaie de paiement) et hors taxes.

4-2-2: *Revision de prix:* Le prix est revise conformément aux dispositions et suivant la formule de revision stipulées aux "CONDITIONS PARTICULIERES".

Les commandes du CONCESSIONNAIRE dont la date de livraison est postérieure à la date de la revision de prix, alors même que la passation des commandes est antérieure à cette date de la revision de prix, sont facturées au prix revisé.

4-2-3: *Conditions de paiement:* La rémunération due au CONCEDANT au titre de chaque commande du CONCESSIONNAIRE sera payable conformément aux dispositions des "CONDITIONS PARTICULIERES" (échéancier de règlement, facturation, modalités de paiement, intérêts de retard).

4-3: **Livraison:**

Le produit contractuel est livré par le CONCEDANT au CONCESSIONNAIRE à

"F.O.B." Aéroport de PARIS (au sens des INCOTERMS 53, Par application directe ou analogique).
Les frais d'emballage sous carton type "transport terrestre et/ou aérien" seront à la charge du CONCEDANT.
Le CONCEDANT, à ses frais et risques, assure le transport du produit contractuel jusqu'au lieu de leur livraison, où la propriété du produit contractuel est transférée au CONCESSIONNAIRE.
Le CONCESSIONNAIRE a la faculté, lors de la livraison de constater ou de faire constater par des mandataires habilités, l'état du produit contractuel ou de son emballage. Si cet examen révèle des défauts ou dommages, le CONCESSIONNAIRE, avant de prendre livraison, devra procéder immédiatement aux réserves d'usage auprès du transporteur et faire parvenir un rapport détaillé au CONCEDANT, qui prendra les mesures appropriées.
A compter de la livraison, le CONCESSIONNAIRE a l'entiére responsabilité, à ses frais et risques, de toutes les opérations nécessaires pour la mise du produit contractuel à la disposition des clients, aux conditions des commandes reçues par lui.

4-4: **Garantie:**

Le CONCEDANT garantie le produit contractuel contre tout vice de fabrication, pendant une période d'un an à compter de la livraison au CONCESSIONNAIRE!
La garantie est limitée au remplacement des pièces défectueuses, à l'exclusion des frais de main d'oeuvre et de transport qui seront mis ou resteront à la charge du CONCESSIONNAIRE.
Les pièces de remplacement ne sont pas garanties.

4-5: **Pièces détachées et matériels de démonstration:**
Le CONCESSIONNAIRE s'engage à acheter au CONCEDANT une certaine quantité de pièces détachées et des matériels de démonstration, conformément aux dispositions inscrites aux "CONDITIONS PARTICULIERES".
Ces pièces détachées et matériels de démonstration sont livrés au CONCESSIONNAIRE dans les conditions de l'article 4-3 ci-dessus.

ARTICLE V — ACTION COMMERCIALE DU CONCESSIONNAIRE:

5-1: **Promotion du produit contractuel et non-concurrence:**
Le CONCESSIONNAIRE s'oblige à promouvoir la vente du produit contractuel avec toute l'efficacité et la diligence attendues d'un bon concessionnaire.
Le CONCESSIONNAIRE s'interdit, pendant toute la durée du présent contrat, de vendre ou de faire vendre tous produits concurrents.
Il s'interdit également de conclure tout accord qui lui conférerait des droits, exclusifs ou non, de représentation d'agence commerciale ou de vente sur les produits mentionnés au paragraphe précédent.

5-2: **Conditions de vente du CONCESSIONNAIRE à ses clients:**
Le CONCESSIONNAIRE arrête, sous sa responsabilité, les conditions générales et/ou particulières applicables à ses ventes à la clientèle.
La rémunération du CONCESSIONNAIRE est constituée par la différence entre le montant de ses ventes à la clientèle et le montant de ses achats au CONCEDANT!

5-3: **Service après-vente et garantie:**

La présente concession de vente comporte l'obligation pour le CONCESSIONNAIRE de fournier a ses clients, à ses frais, un service après-vente régulier et efficace qui permette de sauvegarder la réputation du produit contractuel.

En outre, le CONCESSIONNAIRE est tenu d'accorder à ses clients des conditions de garantie au moins égales à celles données par le CONCEDANT au CONCESSIONNAIRE.

ARTICLE VI — PROPRIETE INDUSTRIELLE:

Le présent contrat ne comporte aucune cession de licence de quelque élément que ce soit des droits de propriété industrielle du CONCEDANT sur le produit contractuel.

Au cas où des tiers feraient valoir vis-à-vis du CONCESSIONNAIRE que la vente du produit contractuel par le CONCEDANT constituerait une contrefaçon de brevets, modèles ou marques leur appartenant, le CONCESSIONNAIRE en avertire immédiate.

Le deux parties examineront ensemble les droits opposés et se prêteront mutuellement et gratuitement l'assistance technique nécessaire a leur défense. Le CONCESSIONNAIRE s'engage à ne pas prendre position vis-à-vis du tiers et notamment à ne pas reconnaître le bien-fondé d'une revendication quelconque, sans avoir obtenu auparavant l'accord du CONCEDANT. En outre, le CONCESSIONNAIRE laissera au CONCEDANT le soin de mener un procès éventuel ou des négociations en vue d'une transaction. Le CONCEDANT prendra en charge les montants dus éventuellement audit tiers au titre de dommages et intérêts ou de rémunération à la suite d'un jugement ou d'une transaction négociée. Les frais résultant d'un procès eventuel seront à la charge du CONCEDANT.

Le CONCESSIONNAIRE informe sans délai le CONCEDANT de toute situation venant à sa connaissance, pouvant constituer une contrefaçon du produit contractuel. Les indemnités ou avantages que le CONCEDANT retirerait des actions éventuellement engagées en conséquence lui deviendraient entièrement acquis.
Le CONCESSIONNAIRE et le CONCEDANT renoncent à tout recours entre eux sur toutes les questions touchant à la propriété industrielle.

ARTICLE VII — RISQUES ET RESPONSABILITES:

Le CONCESSIONNAIRE assume l'entière charge de tous les risques et responsabilités attachés à la commercialisation du produit contractuel, qu'il s'agisse de causes tenant au produit contractuel après sa livraison par le CONCEDANT ou des obligations souscrites par le CONCESSIONNAIRE envers ses clients.

Sous réserve de ses droits à garantie conformément à l'article 4-4 ci-dessus, le CONCESSIONNAIRE renonce à tout recours contre le CONCEDANT.

ARTICLE VIII — FISCALITE:

Le CONCESSIONNAIRE fera son affaire et supportera la charge de toutes les impositions (droits de douanes, taxes, impôts, redevances etc . . .) qui seraient dues, hors de FRANCE, en relation avec les opérations et les transactions réalisées dans le cadre du présent contrat.

Dans le cas où de telles impositions viendraient à être levées sur le CONCEDANT, le CONCESSIONNAIRE mettra en temps utile à sa disposition les fonds nécessaires pour leur réglement.

Les parties se concerteront périodiquement, en tant que de besoin, sur l'application des dispositions ci-dessus.

ARTICLE IX — CESSION:

Le CONCEDANT et le CONCESSIONNAIRE, respectivement, ne pourront céder à des tiers leurs droits et obligations au titre du présent contrat, qu'avec l'accord préalable et écrit de l'autre partie. Par dérogation à ce principe, le CONCEDANT pourra céder librement ses droits et obligations à toute entreprise ayant une participation dans son capital ou dans le capital de laquelle le CONCEDANT a une participation, dans les deux cas directement ou indirectement.

ARTICLE X — DUREE — RESILIATION:

Le présent contrat entre en vigueur à la date de sa signature pour une période probatorire de Il se renouvelle ensuite par tacite reconduction pour une ou plusieurs périodes successives d'une durée ..... chacune.

Le contrat pourra être résillié à la fin de chaque période, à l'initiative de l'une ou l'autre des parties sous réserve, pour la partie qui désire résilier, d'informer l'autre partie de son intention au moins ..... à l'avance et par écrit.

En complément de ces dispositions, il sera fait application, le cas échéant, des stipulations suivantes: Le contrat sera résiliable à la fin de chaque période annuelle et sans préavis, si le nombre des commandes passées par le CONCESSIONNAIRE au cours des douze mois qui précèdent n'a pas atteint le niveau prévu par l'article 4-1 ci-dessus et les dispositions des "CONDITIONS PARTICULIERES" s'y rapportant. Le contrat sera résiliable à tout moment en cas de manquement grave de l'une des parties dans l'exécution de ses obligations, dès lors que la partie défaillante, sans justifier d'un empêchement constitutif d'un cas de force majeure, n'exécuterait pas effectivement les obligations en cause dans le délai de 30 jours suivant la mise en demeure expresse faite par l'autre partie.

Le contrat sera résilié de plein droit en cas de cessation définitive d'activité de l'une ou l'autre des parties, notamment par suite de liquidation des biens.

ARTICLE II — LIQUIDATION DU CONTRAT:

11-1: **Commandes en cours:**

En règle générale, les commandes passées par le CONCESSIONNAIRE au CONCEDANT avant la date de résiliation seront exécutées jusqu'à leur terme, dans les conditions définies au présent contrat. Le CONCESSIONNAIRE s'engage à accepter les livraisons effectuées, sur la base de ces commandes, après la date de résiliation.

Toutefois, en cas de résiliation pour manquement grave du CONCESSIONNAIRE, le CONCEDANT se réserve le droit d'arrêter ses livraisons à la date de la résiliation.

D'autre part, en cas de résiliation de plein droit comme spécifié au dernier alinéa de l'article 10, les livraisons seront toujours arrêtées à la date de la résiliation.

Dans les deux situations indiquées ci-dessus, la reddition des comptes entre les parties sera effectuée en fonction des livraisons réalisées jusqu' à la data de la résiliation du contrat.

11-2: **Indemnisation:**

Nonobstant toute disposition contraire, la résiliation du présent contrat, pour quelque cause que ce soit, ne pourra en aucun cas donner lieu à une quelconque indemnisation entre les parties.

ARTICLE 12 — DROIT APPLICABLE — REGIMENT DES LITIGES —

L'interprétation et l'exécution du présent contrat seront soumises au droit francais.

En cas de différend, les parties s'efforceront de

définir une solution amiable en sollicitant éventuellement l'avis, qui ne les liera point, d'un expert désigne en commun. A défaut d'accord, le litige sera déferé devant les Tribunaux du lieu du Siège Social du CONCEDANT, qui seront seuls compétents.

Date

Lieu

CONCEDANT,	CONCESSIONNAIRE,
(signature)	(signature)

CONDITIONS PARTICULIERES

— Produit contractuel
— Territoire de Vente
— Quota de Vente
— Prix

- Montant
- Date d'établissement
- Revision de prix
- Conditions de paiement
    - Echéancier
    - Facturation
    - Modalités de paiement
    - Intérêts de retard

— Pièces détachées et matériels de démonstration
— Disposition diverses (compléments ou dérogations au CONDITIONS GENERALES).

Date

Lieu

CONCEDANT, CONCESSIONNAIRE

(signature) (signature)

Appendix 2

Example of a company participating in an exhibition in the USSR

Taking part in an exhibition in a country in Eastern Europe and particularly in the USSR is very different from taking part in one in Great Britain, France, or West Germany. The British exhibitor may be surprised by the way in which the exhibition is organised. Once he has been invited to the Soviet Union he must be prepared to comply with all the country's rules and regulations. In order to confirm that he will be welcomed at the exhibition he must make enquiries at the Russian commercial delegation in Britain, at the central purchasing offices and at the Anglo-Soviet Chamber of Commerce. Another method, which can be used in conjunction with the first, is to send about a dozen dossiers on the company and its products to the relevant Soviet central purchasing office, which will then pass on this information to the potential customers, where such a purchase has been planned, or is at least a possibility. Normally it is almost impossible for the potential customers to meet the exporter but, in this way, they are invited to the exhibition by the central purchasing offices and the chances of selling their merchandise are therefore increased.

In our example, Paton contacts the Soviet Chamber of Commerce in order to obtain the relevant forms for participating in the exhibition. Once these forms have been filled in (requests for participation, interpreters, surface area required etc.), they must be sent to the General Directorate of Fairs and Exhibitions in the USSR, together with a proforma invoice for the merchandise to be exhibited.

What merchandise to take?

Choosing what merchandise to exhibit depends on the amount that has to be transported as well as the actual merchandise itself. The Russian customers have *fair credits,* i.e. a particular sum which can be spent buying merchandise at an exhibition. These credits, which are valid only for exhibited goods, at least in principle, cannot be used to buy goods which have to be dispatched at a later date, by the exporter. Therefore, it is necessary to make enquiries about what merchandise could interest the Russian customers and the likely number of potential customers. Although this last point might be practically impossible to find out, Paton could make enquiries at the central purchasing office for advice on the quantity of merchandise to take to the exhibition.

The proforma invoice

The proforma invoice is the basic document in any transaction at an exhibition. The central purchasing offices only buy goods during an exhibition if the exporter is in a position to give them discounts based on the fact that the goods have been exhibited, whether they have been or not, i.e. if they have been stored in a warehouse. In calculating the price he is going to charge, Paton must provide for a negotiating margin of between 5 and 12 per cent. Also the transportation and insurance costs should appear separately on the proforma invoice. It is advisable to treat this sum as a loss and to include it as an additional discount to the customer. In fact, it is very difficult to recoup this cost when the merchandise is sold, as the buyers feel that any unsold goods should be returned to Britain. Therefore not only will the cost of the outward journey be a net loss for the exporter but so will the return journey.

The authorities at the exhibition will return form No. 1 (request for participation) when they have agreed to Paton's inclusion in the VISOTECHNIKA exhibition. Paton should then actively prepare for the exhibition.

Expenses incurred

Paton does not have a continuous flow of business with the USSR and knows very little about the sales opportunities there. The ECGD, by means of a comprehensive insurance, offers him the possibility, on the one hand, of limiting his financial risks in case of bankruptcy and, on the other hand, of providing half the real costs during a two-year period without any interest. The ECGD fairs and exhibitions guarantee is a real help to British exporters and in particular to small and medium-sized companies which usually have limited resources and which very often only have hypothetical assurances of sales.

Costs of hiring the stand : These are specified when a stand is requested. Below we give a guide to the tariffs usually charged for stands in the USSR for an exhibition of about 10 days in duration.

(1974 tariffs.)

Price per sq. metre/International exhibitions

Covered area	£11.25
Uncovered area	£ 4.50
Covered warehouse	£ 4.50
Open air warehouse	£ 3.00

Price per sq. metre/National and foreign exhibitions for a period of 30 days

Covered area	£ 6.75
Uncovered area	£ 3.75
Covered warehouse	£ 3.00
Open air warehouse	£ 2.25

Costs of equipping the stand : All these costs can be calculated from the prices shown on the request forms for material and labour.

Proforma Invoice enclosed with request for participation in the Visotechnica Exhibition.

PATON SYSTEMS,
ENGLAND ROAD,
LONDON, NE1 9LP

USSR 107232, MOSCOW
SOKOLNICHESKY VAL 1-A
General Directorate of
Exhibitions in the U.S.S.R.
1974 VISOTECHNICA EXHIBITION
FEBRUARY 20, 1974

INVOICE NO:
PROFORMA

QUANTITY	DESCRIPTION	UNIT PRICE	TOTAL
3	Recorders no.2205	10.00	30.00
3	Recorders no.2206	8.00	24.00
3	Oscilloscopes	9.50	28.50
45	Relays 310/324	30	13.50
3	Television cameras no. 530258	12.00	36.00
30	Films ref. 18 for camera no. 530258	55	16.50
60	Films ref. 12 for camera no. 530258	66	39.60
	Transportation		4.80
	Total		192.90
	Price before Tax CIF Moscow		
	Total weight including packaging 900 kg.		
	Total volume: $2.3m^3$		

BANK: NATIONAL WESTMINSTER BANK

ACCOUNT NO ....

Example of the Paton System's Stand

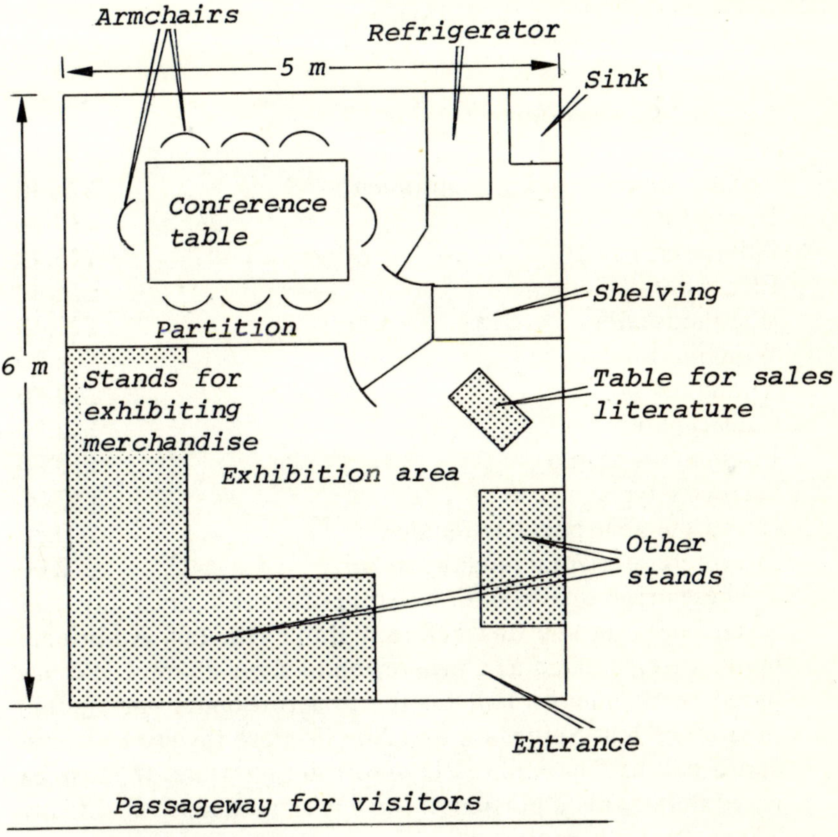

Our exporter's stand does not have the prestige of a stand belonging to a multinational company, but it does have the advantage of being fairly cheap to set up. Also, in the USSR it is not usually a good idea for the exhibitor to have too ostentatious a stand. In our example, Paton Systems has leased the equipment from the authorities at the exhibition. Another more costly method is to deal with companies which specialise in installing stands in the USSR. However, the exporter will have to add an extra 20 per cent to the estimated cost of setting up the stand because of the many additional expenses which occur for practically everything on the site. Below we give a guide to the principal expenses incurred in setting up a stand in the USSR.

Labour/Price per day

Technician to install the equipment	£15.40
Decorator	£17.70
Painter-carpenter	£15.40
Electrician-plumber	£15.40
Warehouseman	£15.40
Watchman	£ 6.00
Attendant	£10.50
Cameraman	£12.80
Fireman (24 hours)	£18.00
Secretary-typist	£ 7.90
Interpreter (European languages)	£10.50
Interpreter (Oriental languages)	£12.00

These prices are valid for a period of eight hours a day, and seven hours on any day before a Bank Holiday. Additional hours are calculated as a proportion of these charges and are based on time and a half for the first two hours and double time after that. Saturdays and Sundays are invoiced at time and a half and national holidays at double time. It must be noted that if only a portion of the day is worked, the company is invoiced for a whole day.

Once Paton has decided to set up its stand itself it must call on local labour actually to install it. Even restricting costs to the maximum he will still need an electrician-plumber, carpenter-painter and a warehouseman just for putting the stand up and taking it down, i.e. a total cost of £92.40. The electrician will need to work for about an hour to install the electric points, and the painter-carpenter for about two hours. Because of the high costs for the work to be done, some forwarding agents take charge of hiring these workmen and recoup the costs from their customers in proportion to the time they are used. The advantage to the exporter is obvious and the problems of finding these workmen are allayed. Also it is easier for the exporter to deal in English with his forwarding agent on the spot than with the authorities at the exhibition.

Construction materials

Wood (pine, deal etc.)
Plywood
Cement
Linoleum
Nails
Petrol
Paraffin for tractors
Motor oil
Zinc
Frosted glass
Concrete and asphalt flooring
Laying floor tiles
Water pipes
Electric cables
Wood varnish
Electric signs

Various pieces of equipment that can be rented

Compressor
Tables
Low tables for sales literature
Chairs
Armchairs
Wooden or metal filing
Carpet
Typewriters
Refrigerator
Coat-stand

TELEPHONE
Main apparatus
Extensions
Installation of a local communications system on a contractual basis:
ELECTRICITY AND WATER
Lighting
Other
Water

Transport costs : Paton decides to send its merchandise by road and engages the services of a firm specialising in transporting merchandise to exhibitions in the USSR. The costs of transportation, packaging and insurance depend on the charges of the particular company concerned.
Travel and accommodation expenses: The exporter would benefit from asking his local travel agent to supply him with a 'fair contract' (aeroplane + hotel + internal travel) rather than a separate airplane ticket and hotel reservation in Moscow which would be more expensive. In our example the two representatives of the Paton company are tsaying for three weeks. In fact one should arrive at least two days before the exhibition begins and stay for two or three days after it ends.
Advertising and promotional expenses : Advertising expenses, which are often difficult to determine, can only be estimated roughly. These expenses include:
Sales literature.
Films and transparencies to be shown at the exhibition.

Gadgets to be given to visitors to the stand and to customers. These gadgets play an important role, particularly in the USSR and the exporter should never forget to take them with him. They may be in the form of lighters, key-rings, pens and emblems, all engraved with the name of the exporting company. Any company which does not have any gadgets to give to his customers is usually thought of as a 'poor' company.

Drinks, alcohol and cigarettes to be offered or consumed during the exhibition. In the USSR champagne and lighttobacco cigarettes are much appreciated. Some forwarding agents which specialise in fairs and exhibitions, supply their customers with spirits and cigarettes at favourable rates, known as 'exhibition export tariffs'.

Lectures. The exporter will be able to give lectures on his products at an exhibition. Unlike exhibitions in Western Europe these lectures, which are planned at the beginning of the exhibition, are often attended by large as well as specialist audiences. The cost of a two-hour lecture, with a hall, an interpreter, slides etc. is about £90. Paton will benefit from holding this lecture because of the impact it can have on an audience. It will be as well if the exporter prepares the text of the lecture before he goes to the USSR as it will have to be sent to the authorities at the exhibition before it starts.

The costs of advertising in the exhibition's catalogue. A page will probably cost £150 and half a page £75.

Financial assistance: Although the cost of exhibitng abroad seems at first to be rather high, the British government, through the BOTB, will usually help exporters in the following ways.

A specialist department of the BOTB, 'the Fairs and Promotions Branch', may suggest sites which have favourable rates for British exporters wishing to exhibit abroad at fairs where there will be British participants.

These rates vary between approximately £3 and £6 depending on whether the stand is covered or not. However, as these rates are rather low, it means that the area of the stand will rarely be more than fifteen square metres. Naturally, a large stand will cost more to hire than that.

The travel costs for two representatives of a company which is exhibiting, as well as for two representatives of the company actually organising the British exhibition abroad, are assumed by the BOTB in the case of exhibitions outside Western Europe, where the sum does not exceed 50 per cent of the cost of the normal economy flight. In the case of an exhibition taking place outside Western Europe, the BOTB also engages to pay 50 per cent of the cost of the return freightage of goods not sold at the exhibition provided that these goods are dispatched to Great Britain direct within the year following the end of the exhibition.

Dispatch of goods

The dispatch of goods to the exhibition must be carefully planned by the exporter. Paton should pay special attention to the quality of the packaging as the goods will be handled a great deal. The various pieces of merchandise should be packed in packing cases and not in cardboard boxes. In fact, each packing case should be able to be used again for sending the merchandise back to Britain should it not be sold at the exhibition, or even for delivering the goods to the customer if they are sold. It is almost impossible to find the necessary packing materials on the site.

Office supplies will be equally difficult to find. Paton should therefore ensure that he takes everything that may be required during the exhibition such as cellotape, scissors, stapler, drawing pins, paper, calculator etc.

One would imagine that all articles of the same nature would be packed together but as Paton can only exhibit a portion of his merchandise and must store the rest in a warehouse, he should put his demonstration goods together in certain cases and put everything which is to be stored into other cases so that it can go through customs duty-free. In this way he will not have to open all the cases to find his demonstration goods. Furthermore, it is very difficult to store open cases and Paton will be using most of his stand for storing the merchandise. Although this may seem obvious one still often sees many exporters at exhibitions in countries in Eastern Europe filling their stands with goods which could have been stored, because they have not taken the precaution of distributing their merchandise properly in the various cases. These cases should be carefully numbered and labelled. The labelling must be clear and easy to understand. Some forwarding agents send their customers standard labels. The label must be written in block capitals and it is always better to put two labels on a case rather than one.

Example of a label on a package going to exhibition

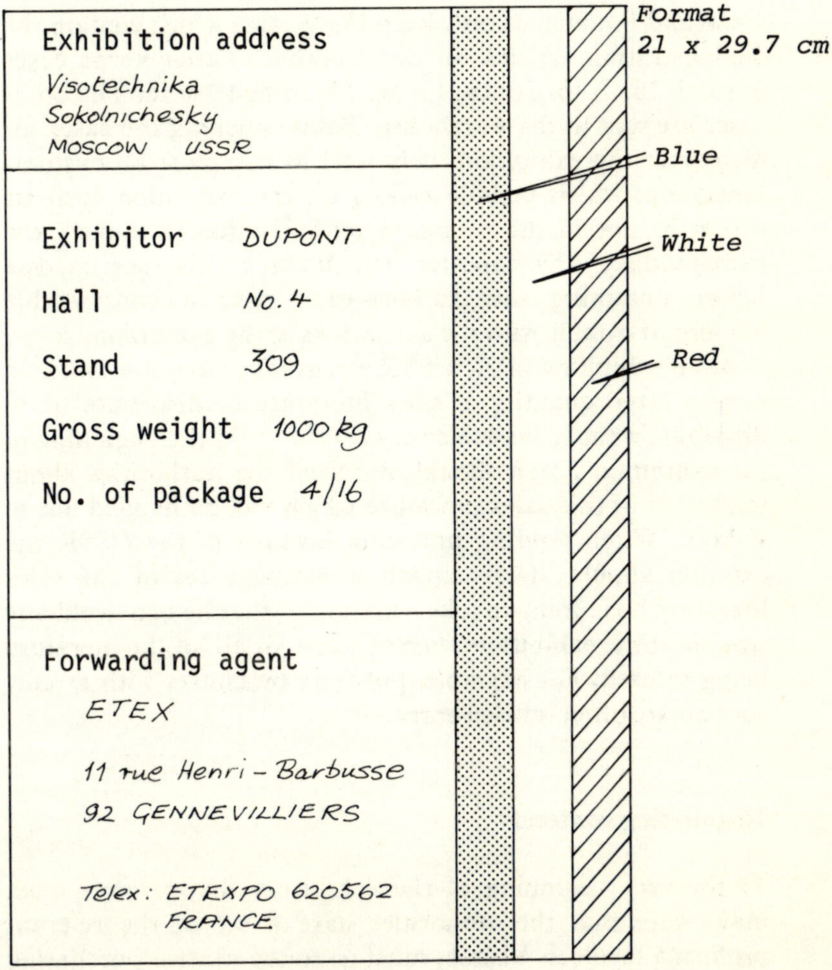

When sending his merchandise to the forwarding agent, Paton must attach a packing list and the proforma invoices, which can be on the same (and only) document (see example below).

The exhibition itself

When the merchandise arrives in Moscow it is taken to the stand and Paton need only keep those cases which contain the demonstration articles. In our example, Paton keeps cases 3/16, 4/16, 7/16, 10/16, 13/16, 15/16 and 16/16. The other cases are sent to the warehouse. Before opening the cases for display at the exhibition, it is vital to complete all customs formalities which include calling on the exhibition customs officer to obtain the necessary authorisation to unpack the merchandise. Any exporter who unpacks his merchandise before obtaining this authorisation risks a considerable amount of trouble with the authorities at the exhibition.

At an exhibition in the USSR it is usually advisable either to have a large quantity of sales literature to distribute or to distribute what is available very carefully. At the beginning of the exhibition Paton should also send the authorities about ten copies of this sales literature which will be handed out to visitors. When sending proforma invoices to the USSR the exporter should always attach a complete set of the sales literature he is going to take with him so that he can avoid any trouble at the exhibition, such as some, or all, of the literature being refused. For example, publicity brochures with a reply coupon are often refused entry.

Negotiating contracts

At the very beginning of the exhibition the exporter must make sure that the authorities have a set of the relevant proforma invoices. Visitors must go to the central purchasing office to pick up the reference numbers and prices of the exhibits they wish to see. If the proforma invoices are not registered with the central purchasing office the customer

PROFORMA INVOICE FOR THE VISOTECHNICA EXHIBITION IN MOSCOW

EXHIBITOR:
ADDRESS: HALL NO:
TELEPHONE: IN CHARGE OF DEPARTURE:
TELEX: IN CHARGE OF STAND:

TRADE NAME AND NO. ON EACH CASE	WEIGHT NET	WEIGHT GROSS	SIZE	CONTENTS	FOB PRICE £

cannot request to purchase this merchandise at the office. The exporter should also find out which offices are responsible for purchasing his goods. At the end of the exhibition officials from these offices will visit the stands with a view to negotiating contracts. The exporter must be very patient. Exhibitors can rarely pride themselves with having signed any contracts before the last day of the exhibition. Moreover, a great many only sign within a few hours of their plane taking off, after having spent several days discussing the discount on which the whole transaction is based.

The contract is drawn up in English, German or French. A certificate of acceptance and receipt must be attached to this contract. As stated in all contracts, this document is always necessary in obtaining payment for the goods. Usually the USSR Bank of External Commerce effects payment within 30 days of the following documents being received by them:

— copy of the bill of sale;
— invoices;
— certificate of acceptance and receipt signed by both parties;
— certificate of quality for the goods sold;
— any other documents specified in the contract.

Appendix 3

Selected books dealing with exports

General Works

Export Handbook
published by British Overseas Trade Board
Export: A Manual of Instruction
by Antony W. Masson Business Books, London
International Marketing
by K.A. Yarker Business Books, London
Exportmanship: a career in export
by Hamish Lindsay. Educational Explorers. Reading.
Businessman's guide to the centrally planned economy countries
edited by S. Black. Modino Press.
Case studies in export organisation
by Andrew Duguid and Elliot Jaques, Department of Trade and Industry.
Exhibiting Overseas: a marketing shop window
by S. Black. Pitman
Exhibitions: universal marketing tools
by A. Alles. Cassell/Associated Business Programmes Ltd.
Businessman's guide to the Common Market
by D. Prag and E.D. Nicholson, Pall Mall.
Export — Import in four languages
by H.E. Horten, Gower Press, London.

Distribution and Sales

Export salesmanship
by John Frain. 175 pages, 1970. Available from United Commercial Travellers Association, Bexton Lane, Knutsford, Cheshire.
Export agents
by Colin McMillan and Sydney Paulden. Gower Press, London
Salesmanship and salesforce management
by Edward G. Bursk and G. Scott Hutchison, Harvard Business School
International marketing
John Fayerweather Holt Rinhart and Winston, New York

Banking

Documentary credits: uniform customs and practice for documentary credits
(ICC brochure 222): British National Committee, International Chamber of Commerce.

Customs

Transportation

Legislation

Guide to ICC arbitration
British National Committee, International Chamber of Commerce, High Holborn House, 52-54 High Holborn, London WC1V 6SW
The export trade: the law and practice of international trade
by C.M. Schmitthoff
International guide to company formation
(ICC brochure 263). British National Committee, International Chamber of Commerce, High Holborn House, 52-54 High Holborn, London WC1V 6SW

Incoterms
la Chambre de Commerce Internationale

Useful addresses for the exporter

BASEEFA (BRITISH APPROVALS SERVICE FOR ELECTRICAL EQUIPMENT IN FLAMMABLE ATMOSPHERES) Harpur Hill, Buxton, Derbyshire SK17 9JN (*tel* Buxton 6211)
BRITISH CALIBRATION SERVICE 26 Chapter Street, London SW1P 4NS (*tel* 01-834 7032)
BRITISH CONSULTANTS BUREAU 55-58 Pall Mall, London SW1Y 5LH (*tel* 01-839 7687 *telex* 916469 for BRITBURO (a/b CONSAMACH))
BRITISH EXPORT HOUSES ASSOCIATION 69 Cannon Street, London EC4N 5AB (*tel* 01-248 4444)
BBX EXTERNAL SERVICES Editor, Science, Industry and Exports, Bush House, Strand, London WC2B 4PH (*tel* 01-240 3456, ext 2471 *telex* 22182 BBC London) and you nearest BBC Regional Office (see page 170 for addresses)
THE BRITISH OVERSEAS TRADE BOARD 1 Victoria Street, London SW1H 0ET (*tel* 01-215 7877 *telex* 27366 DTIHQ London)
BRITISH STANDARDS INSTITUTION 2 Park Street, London W1A 2BS (*tel* 01-629 9000 *telex* 266933 BSI London) and at Maylands Avenue, Hemel Hempstead, Herts (*tel* Hemel Hempstead 3111 *telex* 82424 BSI HEMEL)
CENTRAL OFFICE OF INFORMATION (COI) (Headquarters) Hercules Road, Wesminster Bridge Road, London SE1 7DU (*tel* 01-928 2345 *telex* 915444 CENTROFORM Ldn) or your nearest Government Information office (for addresses see page 176-177)
CHARTERED INSTITUTE OF PATENT AGENTS Staple Inn Buildings, High Holborn, London WC1V 7PZ (*tel* 01-405 9450)
CONFEDERATION OF BRITISH INDUSTRY 21 Tothill Street, London SW1H 9LP (*tel* 01-930 6711 *telex* 21332 COBUSTRY London)
THE CROWN AGENTS FOR OVERSEAS GOVERNMENTS AND ADMINISTRATIONS 4 Millbank London SW1P 3JD (*tel* 01-222 7730 *telex* 916205 CROWN London)
DESIGN COUNCIL 28 Haymarket, London SW1Y 4SU (*tel* 01-839 8000)
DESIGN COUNCIL SCOTTISH COMMITTEE 72 St Vincent Street, Glasgow G2 5TN (*tel* 041-221 6121)

EXPORT CREDITS GUARANTEE DEPARTMENT Aldermanbury House, Aldermanbury, London EC2P 2EL (*tel* 01-606 6699 *telex* 883601 ECGDHQ Ldn)

EXPORT LICENSING BRANCH Department of Trade, Sanctuary Buildings, 16-20 Great Smith Street, London SW1P 3DB (*tel* 01-215 5718 *telex* 27366/917929 DTIHQ London)

EXPORT SERVICES AND PROMOTIONS DIVISION Export House, 50 Ludgate Hill, London EC4M 7HU (**tel** 01-248 5757 **telex** 886143 DTI Export Ldn)

FAIRS AND PROMOTIONS BRANCH Hillgate House, 26 Old Bailey, London EC4M 7HU (*tel* 01-248 5757 *telex* 886143 DTI Export Ldn)

HM CUSTOMS AND EXCISE (General Customs Division) Kent House, Upper Ground, London SE1 9PP (*tel* 01-928 0533)

HM CUSTOMS AND EXCISE King's Beam House, Mark Lane, London EC3R 7HE (*tel* 01-626 1515 *telex* 886231 CUSEX HQ Ldn)

INSTITUTE OF EXPORT World Trade Centre, London E1 9AA (*tel* 01-790 7979)

INSTITUTE OF FREIGHT FORWARDERS LTD Suffield House, 9 Paradise Road, Richmond, Surrey TW9 1SA (*tel* 01-948 3141)

THE INSTITUTE OF LINGUISTS Lloyds Bank Chambers, 91 Newington Causeway, London SE1 6BN (*tel* 01-407 4755/6)

INSTITUTE OF MARKETING Moor Hall, Cookham, Berks SL6 9QH (*tel* Bourne End 24922)

INSTITUTE OF TRADE MARK AGENTS 69 Cannon Street, London EC4N 5AB (*tel* 01-248 4444)

LONDON COURT OF ARBITRATION OF THE LONDON CHAMBER OF COMMERCE AND INDUSTRY AND THE CITY CORPORATION 69 Cannon Street, London, EC4N 5AB (*tel* 01-248 4444 *telex* 888941 CHAMCOM London)

MANAGEMENT CONSULTANTS ASSOCIATION 23-24 Cromwell Place, London SW7 2LG (*tel* 01-584 7283)

METRICATION BOARD 22 Kingsway, London WC2B 6LE (*tel* 01-242 6828)

OVERSEAS TARIFFS AND REGULATIONS SECTION (OTAR) Export Data Branch, Export House, 50 Ludgate Hill, London EC4M 7HU (*tel* 01-248 5757 *telex* 886143 DTI EXPORT Ldn)

PATENT OFFICE 25 Southampton Buildings, London WC2A 1AY (*tel* 01-405 8721)

PIRA Research Association for the Paper and Board, Printing and Packaging Industries, Randalls Road, Leatherhead, Surrey KT22 7RU (*tel* Leatherhead 76161 *telex* 929810 PIRA LEATHERHD)

SIMPLIFICATION OF INTERNATIONAL TRADE PROCEDURES (SITPRO) BOARD 26-32 Caxton Street, London SW1H 0RJ (*tel* 01-222 3673/4/5 *telex* 919130 SITPRO Ldn)

THE SCIENCE REFERENCE LIBRARY (Holborn Branch), 25 Southampton Buildings, London WC2A 1AW (*tel* 01-405 8721)

SCOTTISH EXPORT COMMITTEE Association of Scottish Chambers of Commerce 30 George Square, Glasgow G2 1EQ (*tel* 041-204 2121 *telex* 77667 CHAMBER Glasgow)

STATISTICS AND MARKET INTELLIGENCE LIBRARY and ECONOMICS AND STATISTICS DIVISION (Foreign and Commonwealth Section) Department of Industry both at: Export House, 50 Ludgate Hill, London EC4M 7HU (*tel* 01-248 5757 *telex* 886143 DTI Export Ldn)

STATISTICAL OFFICE (Bill of Entry Section) HM Customs and Excise, Portcullis House, 27 Victoria Avenue, Southend-on-Sea SS2 6AL (*tel* Southend 49421 *telex* 99112 CUSEX Southend)